改革开放*40*周年　江苏住房发展成就文献资料

Achievements of Housing Development in Jiangsu for the 40th Anniversary of the Reform and Opening Up

江苏住房变迁纪实

DOCUMENTARY ON THE EVOLUTION OF RESIDENTIAL HOUSING IN JIANGSU
1978－2017

江苏省住房和城乡建设厅
住宅与房地产业促进中心　主　编

Housing and Real Estate Promotion Center,
Jiangsu Provincial Department of Housing and Urban-Rural Development

南京大学出版社
NANJING UNIVERSITY PRESS

图书在版编目（CIP）数据

江苏住房变迁纪实：1978-2017 / 江苏省住房和城
乡建设厅住宅与房地产业促进中心主编.—南京：南京
大学出版，2018.4
ISBN 978-7-305-20091-5

Ⅰ. ①江… Ⅱ. ①江… Ⅲ. ①住宅建设—概况—江苏
—1978-2017—画册 Ⅳ. ①F299.275.3-64

中国版本图书馆 CIP 数据核字(2018)第 065161 号

出版发行　南京大学出版社
社　　址　南京市汉口路 22 号　　　　　邮　　编　210093
出版人　金鑫荣
书　　名　**江苏住房变迁纪实（1978—2017）**
主　编　江苏省住房和城乡建设厅住宅与房地产业促进中心
责任编辑　束　悦　李　杰　　　　编辑热线　025-83686308

印　　刷　南京碧峰印务有限公司
开　　本　787×1092　　1/12　　印　张　15　　字　数　174 千字
版　　次　2018 年 4 月第 1 版　2018 年 4 月第 1 次印刷
ISBN　978-7-305-20091-5
定　　价　298.00 元（精装）（含光盘）

网　　址　http://www.njupco.com
官方微博　http://weibo.com/njupco
官方微信　njupress
销售热线　025-83594756

主　　　　编　　杜学伦

副　主　编　　赵庆红　　刘向东　　曹云华　　李　强　　陆建生　　徐盛发　　高　枫

执　行　主　编　　徐盛发

总　撰　稿　人　　李　强

责　任　编　辑　　李　堃

编　　　　辑　　陆志刚　　邵　慧　　朱殿君　　黄天昌　　曹又俭

参　编　人　员　　陈文志　　吴立群　　钱　鑫　　康　凯　　冯树云　　陈得生　　任　重　　李　韫　　王双军　　孔　俊

英　文　翻　译　　包亚芝　　朱爱飞　　Nikolas Krause

图片资料提供　　各市县住建、公积金主管部门及档案馆　　陆志刚　　姚克慎　　程　恺　　蒋钰祥　　朱晓光　　陈路昑

　　　　　　　　李　牧　　吴金伟　　李怀大　　滕庆林　　洪晓程　　张良禾　　李　莉　　罡万清　　袁　伟　　陈　着

　　　　　　　　孟　婕　　朱利虎　　向文祥　　金勇兵　　章晓斌　　王　忠　　徐胜振　　万程鹏　　蒋益飞　　雷　鸣

　　　　　　　　刘建华　　丁焕新　　王　昊　　冯　梦　　刘　影　　杨祥富　　戴晶若　　张　娟

前言

　　"安得广厦千万间，大庇天下寒士俱欢颜。"住房是老百姓对美好生活向往的基本需求。改革开放开启了住房建设发展的全新历程，过往的四十年虽在历史长河中相对短暂，但前行的中国住房制度改革，带给了老百姓居住条件的巨大改善以及居住空间、生活方式的巨大变迁，无疑会在中国经济社会发展进程中留下浓墨重彩的一笔。

　　江苏地处东南沿海，是中国改革开放的重要前沿阵地。四十年来，在国家经济体制改革和住房制度改革方针的指引下，江苏人以博大的胸怀、坚韧的品格和坚持不懈的追求，积极探索、勇于实践、大胆创新，率先在全国进行住房制度改革试点，全面实行具有互助性质的住房公积金制度，充分发挥市场对资源的配置作用，住房市场得到快速发展；率先在全省组织开展城镇低收入家庭住房情况调查、出台住房保障行动计划，率先提出构建"系统化设计、制度化安排、规范化建设、长效化推进"的住房保障体系，创新共有产权住房保障模式，住房保障水平持续提升。各级政府坚定不移地承担起住房困难群众保障托底主体责任，解决了 20% 低收入住房困难家庭和外来务工人员基本住房问题，全面实现了"应保尽保"；企业、专业机构和社会组织围绕住房有效供给提供了逐步完善的配套服务，住房供应快速增加，物业服务、养老服务、装饰装修和中介服务市场快速发育逐步规范。结合住房建设发展，江苏始终把人民对美好生活的向往作为奋斗目标，对新建住房更加注重健全功能、提升品质，对既有住宅持续推进有机更新，改善住区环境、完善基础设施和配套服务，住房建设和老百姓的居住服务水平不断提高。2017 年，全省城镇居民人均住房面积比改革开放初期增长了 8 倍多，基本实现了住有所居。2016年，统计部门对全省"民生幸福工程六大体系"公众满意度调查显示，各地群众对住房的满意度位列六项民生工程之首。

《江苏住房变迁纪实（1978—2017）》分为变迁篇、实践篇、展望篇，真实地记录了江苏从"蜗居时代"到"住有所居"的历史变迁，全方位展示了全省各地勇于解放思想、着力破解住房难题所作的积极努力，为我们在新时代实现住房事业高质量发展，提供了重要的参考价值和现实意义。

党的十九大明确"坚持房子是用来住的、不是用来炒的定位，加快建立多主体供给、多渠道保障、租购并举的住房制度"。 习近平总书记对住房工作高度重视并多次作出重要批示指示，2014年年底视察江苏时，对民生工作提出"七个更"的要求，其中就包括"更舒适的居住条件"。这为今后一个时期进一步推动住房发展、做好住房工作指明了方向。江苏将以习近平新时代中国特色社会主义思想为指引，围绕住房工作中仍存在的一些不平衡不充分的发展问题，切实履行好政府保障托底责任，进一步完善住房供应体系，不断探索建立房地产调控长效机制，加快推进"住有所居"向"住有宜居"迈进，为建设"强富美高"新江苏、谱写好新时代中国特色社会主义江苏新篇章作出更大贡献。

编者

2017 年 11 月

Foreword

Where can I get mansions covering thousands of miles that I'd house all scholars poor and make them beam with smiles. Housing is an essential need of people in their pursuit of happy and beautiful life. The reform and opening up started a brand new course for housing development in China. The past four decades, though relatively short in the long history, is undoubtedly an outstanding period in the economic and social development of China as the ongoing housing system reform has brought huge improvement of living conditions and tremendous changes of living space and lifestyle to the Chinese people.

Jiangsu Province, located in the southeast coastal regions, is an important forefront of the reform and opening up in China. In the past four decades, the people in Jiangsu, broadminded and perseverant, have been actively engaged in policy innovation and practices under the guidelines of the state's economic system reform and housing system reform. Jiangsu is one of the first provinces in China that initiated the pilot program of housing system reform. The system of housing provident fund, a policy that allows mutual aid among residents, has been put into application in full scale. The housing market enjoys rapid development as the role of the market has been brought into full play in resource allocation. We take the lead in carrying out the survey on the housing conditions of low-income households and launching the action plan of government-subsidized housing. We also take the lead to develop a government-subsidized housing system that features systematic planning, institutionalized arrangements, standard construction, and long-term promotion. We have started the innovative mode of shared ownership housing and improved the management of government-subsidized housing provision. Governments at all levels remain committed to the housing support for people in difficulties and have provided basic housing for 20% low-income households and migrant workers. Basic subsistence has been realized in full scale for all those people that should be guaranteed. Focusing on effective housing supply, enterprises, specialized institutions, and social organizations are improving their services and the housing supply has been increased rapidly. The markets of realty management, elderly care service, home decoration, and intermediary services are in quick and regulated development. People's pursuit of good life, including better housing, is always the goal of our work in Jiangsu. More attention has been paid to functions and quality of newly built residential housing. Renewal has been carried out to existing residential buildings. Moreover, enhanced residential environment, better infrastructure facilities and supporting services, all contribute to the constant improvement of housing development and service. In 2017, the average floor area per capita of urban residents in Jiangsu increased by more than 8 times than that in the early period of the reform and opening up. The goal of making housing accessible to all people has been basically realized. In a 2016 poll about public satisfaction on the "six major fields of public wellbeing programs" of Jiangsu, it showed that people in the province felt most satisfied with housing.

Documentary on the Evolution of Residential Housing in Jiangsu (1978—2017) consists of three chapters: Changes, Fulfillment, and Future. This book is a true record of historical changes in Jiangsu from the era of humble abode to housing accessible to all people. It shows extensively the efforts that the municipalities throughout the province have taken to free their minds and try to solve tough problems of housing. Their practices, which are meaningful in reality, provide important reference for the high quality housing development that we will realize in the new era.

It has been made clear in the 19th CPC National Congress that we must not forget that housing is for living in, not for speculation and we will move faster to put in place a housing system that ensures supply through multiple sources, provides housing support through multiple channels, and encourages both housing purchase and renting. General Secretary Xin Jinping gives particular attention to the work of housing and has made quite a few important instructions. He set forth seven wishes toward the work of improving people's wellbeing when he visited Jiangsu in 2014. Among these seven wishes, there is "more comfortable living conditions". This instruction shows the direction that we shall follow in the future to further promote housing development and ensure the work is well done. We will follow Xi Jinping Thought on Socialism with Chinese Characteristics for a New Era and effectively perform the government duties to support the disadvantaged as problems caused by unbalanced and inadequate development still exist in the work of housing. We will further improve the housing supply system, keep on exploring the long-term mechanisms to regulate real estate development, accelerate the development from meeting the housing needs of all people to providing liveable housing for all people. We will make greater contributions to the development of a new Jiangsu, which has strong economy, wealthy people, beautiful environment, and enhanced social etiquette and civility, and strive to write a new Jiangsu chapter for the socialism with Chinese characteristics in the new era.

The Editor

November 2017

目录 Contents

第一章 │ 变迁篇
CHAPTER 1 Changes

20世纪70年代末，江苏与全国其他省份一样，经济发展水平不高，居民住房投入严重不足。在知青返城和下放农村回城家庭大量增加等多重因素叠加影响下，百姓住房总体水平处于历史低点，几代人蜗居一室较为普遍，住房质量差、配套差、环境差是那个年代的显著特征。进入80年代后，改革开放浪潮席卷大江南北，住房制度改革多项政策措施在江苏落地生根，为江苏住房事业注入强大动力，住宅小区如雨后春笋拔地而起，在市场机制作用下，快速高效地配置住房资源，在住房公积金制度对住房消费的有效支持下，百姓住房水平快速提升。进入新世纪后，江苏在全国率先构建住房保障体系，以政府有形之手托底保障经济和住房困难家庭，市场和保障相互弥补，相得益彰，到2015年年末，全省基本实现"住有所居"。

During the late 1970s, Jiangsu, like other parts of China, was bothered by an undeveloped economy, including a severe shortage of investment in housing development. Because of the superimposed impact of the considerable increase in the number of educated youth and families turning from the rural areas, the people's housing conditions hit a historical low and it was pretty common that several generations lived in a single room. The poor quality of housing, poor facilities and poor environment constituted the obvious features of buildings of that era. After entering the 1980s, a tide of reform and opening up swept across the country. A string of housing reform policies and measures were implemented in Jiangsu and drove significant development of housing that resulted in a sheer mushrooming of residential quarters. Under the influence of the market, housing resources were allotted in an efficient and effective manner. The strong support of the housing provident fund system on housing consumption helped to improve the people's housing conditions. Entering the new millennium, Jiangsu took the national lead in developing its housing security system to support those families with housing difficulties. The market and the government's subsidization complemented each other to benefit mutually. By the end of 2015, the province had basically achieved the goal of "having housing to live in".

70 年代城市街景
70s Urban Streetscape

住房及配套 | Housing & Infrastructure

70年代——蜗居印象 | 1970s — Crowded Housing

　　改革开放前，在"重生产、轻生活""先生产、后生活"的社会环境下，国家对住房建设的投资渠道单一，主要依靠地方政府土地划拨和财政拨款以及单位自筹资金建设住房，住房极度短缺。各地城镇大部分住房依然是1949年前后建造的1—2层砖木结构住房，设施简陋，两三代人同居一屋的现象十分普遍。在少量新建住房中，以3—4层的砖混结构楼房（俗称筒子楼）最为常见，同一楼层住户共用厨房、厕所等，生活极为不便。一进门槛就是床，马桶水缸一起放，房上吊着一张床，公婆儿媳床靠床。

Before the reform and opening up, in the social environment of "paying more attention to production than living" and "production before living", housing was in extreme shortage. During this period the national investment in housing development simply relied on local governments' land and fiscal allotment, in combination with work units raising of funds independently. Most of the houses in cities and towns throughout the country were the one-storied or two-storied brick-timber houses with poor facilities built around 1949. It was a very most common phenomenon that two or three generations of a family lived in a single room. Of the small number of newly built buildings, the three-storied or four-storied buildings in the brick and mortar structure (commonly known as "tube-shaped apartment") were the most common building style, the families living in those buildings, on the same floor, shared a kitchen, a toilet and so on, living in extreme inconvenience.

常州罗汉路两侧下放回城家庭搭建的简陋棚户房

Shanties put up by the families returning from rural areas on the sides of Luohan Road, Changzhou

南京旧城墙下的"披子房"

"Sheds" put up against the old city wall of Nanjing

1978 年为解决下放回城无房户，常州市政府在浦前北路东侧建设平房 304 间，俗称"南门 300 间"

The Changzhou Municipal Government built simple housing (commonly known as "South Gate 300 Rooms") in an integrated manner to solve the housing difficulties of the returned educated youth

泰州老电视塔北片街区　The block to the north of the old TV tower in Taizhou

苏州山塘街民居
Shantang Street folk houses, Suzhou

扬州文昌阁小三元巷街景　Wenchangge Xiaosanyuan Lane street view, Yangzhou

两代人同居一室
Two generations living in one room

以平房为主的常州民居
One-storey houses were dominant in Changzhou

泰州海陵路大林桥民居及其配套
Hailing Road Dalinqiao folk houses and
infrastructure, Taizhou

间距狭窄的筒子楼
Tube-shaped apartment buildings with small spacing

筒子楼住户搬家场景
Dwellers living in tube-shaped apartments in the process of moving

京杭大运河无锡段江尖民居　Jiangjian folk houses at Wuxi Section of Beijing-Hangzhou Grand Canal

淮安市清江大闸口民居
Qingjiang Dazhakou folk houses, Huai'an

泰州稻河沿河民居　*Folk houses along the Daohe River, Taizhou*

煤球店
Briquettes shop

狭窄简陋的厨房
A simple kitchen with poor facilities

住户在煤炉上做饭
Cooking by a coal stove

喜搬液化气瓶
Carrying LPG cylinders home joyfully

徐州现存筒子楼——庆祝楼　　Tube-shaped apartment building — Qingzhu Building, Xuzhou

共用厨房　Sharing the kitchen

共用盥洗间　Sharing the washroom

公共厕所　Public toilet

居民取用井水洗菜的生活场景
Cleaning food with water from a well

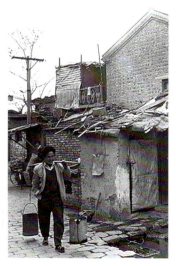

公共水龙头边洗衣服
Doing washing near a public tap

南京老城南水井
Well in the old city of Nanjing

从供水点挑水回家
Carrying water home from the water supply room

居民区的老虎灶
"Tiger-shaped" stove (for large-scale boiling of water) in the residential area

送水上门的开水车
Door-to-door delivery of hot water

住户每天到开水站打开水
Fetching hot water from the supply room

大杂院里聚餐情景
A communal meal

房前屋后，大杂院里，邻里交流频繁，亲如一家
Many families share a yard in familiar proximity

集体包饺子
Making dumplings together

相伴嬉戏不知返
Playing happily

洋画拍出大赢家
Playing picture cards

小人书里乾坤大
Reading picture books with passion

舞刀弄剑争霸王
Sword against sword

夏日竹床纳凉爽
Playing chess in a bamboo bed

筒子楼电表箱
Electrometer boxes mounted on a tube-shaped apartment building

运送粪便
Delivery dejecta from public toilets

路边垃圾箱
Roadside garbage container

收费公厕
Fee-paying public toilet

马桶洗刷和晾晒
Washing and drying chamber pots

湖滨菜场蔬菜酱品部开业剪彩
Opening ceremony of Hubing vegetable market

幼儿园
Kindergarten

马路边的早点摊  Breakfast vendors on the street

小区外马路菜市场
Vegetables sold on the
street market

南京鼓楼广场　Drum Tower Square, Nanjing

盐城建军路　Jianjun Road of Yancheng

公交车站
Bus station

拥挤的公交车
A crowded bus

南京火车站　Nanjing Railway Station

淮安清江大闸口
Huai'an Qingjiang Dazhakou

出租车　Taxi

市民广场
Citizen square

80 年代城市街景
80s Urban Streetscape

80 年代 —— 小区初妆 | 1980s —— Debut of Residential Quarters

进入 80 年代，由于大批知青、下放户回城，住房短缺问题十分突出，各地政府把住房问题放到重要位置来抓。常州市率先采用综合开发、配套建设的方式建造住宅小区，为解决住房问题探索新路子。这一时期建设的住宅多为 5—6 层的成套住宅，中小套面积 40—60 平方米，大套 70—80 平方米，小区内生活配套设施基本齐全。

When it came to the 1980s, the return to cities of a large number of educated youth and families from the rural areas intensified the housing shortage and forced governments at all levels to give priority to solving the housing difficulties. Changzhou City pioneered in carrying out comprehensive development of residential quarters and construction of supporting facilities, which provided a way to solve the housing crisis. The residential buildings built in the 1980s were dominated by complete sets of five-storied or six-storied buildings, ranging from 40—60 square meters in smaller houses and the large houses ranging from 70—80 square meters. These residential quarters were equipped with basically complete service facilities.

1981 年 1 月竣工的常州花园新村是全省最早实行的"统一规划、征地、设计、投资、施工、分配和管理"（即"六统一"）建设的住宅小区

Changzhou Huayuan Xincun built up in January 1981 was Jiangsu's earliest residential quarter adopting unified planning, land requisition, design, investment, construction, distribution and management, and all supporting facilities were put into service together with the buildings

80年代中后期，省和南京市政府斥巨资建成了当时全国规模最大的住宅小区——南湖小区，集中解决了南京市知青和下放回城人员的住房困难及城市居住环境脏乱差问题

In the middle and late 1980s, the Provincial Government and the Nanjing Municipal Government spent huge sums of money to build up the then largest residential quarter nationwide, the Nanhu Residential Quarter that solved the housing difficulties of the educated youth and their families returning from rural areas to Nanjing and improved the living conditions of the poor urban dwellers in a centralized manner

南通城南新村住宅小区　Chengnan Xincun Residential Quarter, Nantong

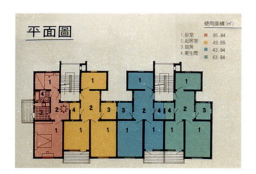

平面圖

使用面积（㎡）

1. 卧室　35.84
2. 起居室　49.55
3. 厨房　43.94
4. 衛生間　43.94

代表性户型图　Representative blueprint

泰州镇北住宅小区
Zhenbei Residential Quarter, Taizhou

全省最早实行物业管理的住宅小区——
常州红梅新村

*Hongmei Xincun, Changzhou — Jiangsu's first residential
quarter adopting property management*

开始注重景观绿化建设的住宅小区——
徐州湖滨新村

*Hubin Xincun, Xuzhou — the residential quarter marking
the start of emphasis on landscaping*

最早开展住房制度改革试点企业江苏宿迁玻璃厂集体宿舍

Jiangsu Suqian Glass Factory Dormitory — the earliest enterprise piloting the housing system reform

机关企事业单位干部职工宿舍楼

Staff dormitory of a government institution

工业厂房、职工宿舍及配套生活设施同时规划同步建设的典型项目——仪征化纤集团职工宿舍

Staff Quarters of Yizheng Chemical Fiber Group — a typical project on synchronized planning and construction of industrial premises, staff quarters and supporting living facilities

吃饭时客厅变成了餐厅　The living room also serving as a dining room

客厅里的生活　Life in the living room

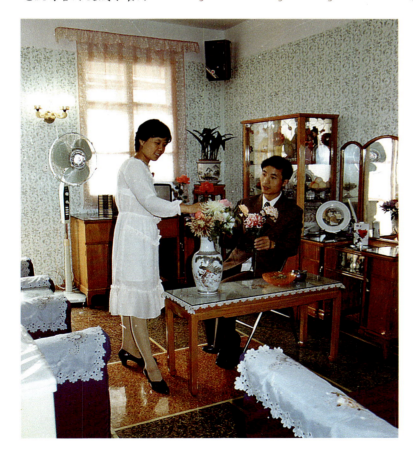

重要的文娱场所——舞厅
An important recreational venue
— dance hall

时髦的婚房装修：墙纸、地板革、马赛克磁砖
Trendy decoration for newlyweds: Wallpaper, PVC floor leather, mosaic tiles

住区配套 Residential district facilities

小区幼儿园　Kindergarten of the quarter

小区文化站　Cultural station of the quarter

小区商场
Store of the quarter

小区自行车库
Bicycle garage of the quarter

南京地标性建筑——金陵饭店　Jinling Hotel, a landmark building in Nanjing

泰州第一百货商店
Taizhou No. 1 Department Store

小商品批发市场
Wholesale market for small commodities

工人文化宫和工人电影院
Workers' Cultural Palace and Workers' Cinema

公用电话亭
Public telephone booth

90 年代城市街景
90s Urban Streetscape

90 年代 —— 春到住区 | 1990s —— Flourishing Housing Development

　　改革开放进入 90 年代，江苏住房建设快速发展。苏州桐芳巷旧城改造、常州红梅西村小区、南京龙江高教公寓等，成为这一时期住宅小区建设的代表。各地政府建设了大批安居工程住宅小区，用于住房解困解危。90 年代中后期，小高层、高层住宅开始出现，设计、施工采用国家推广的"四新"技术，住宅品质进一步提高。住房困难得到大大缓解。

　　When the reform and opening up entered the 1990s, Jiangsu enjoyed rapid development of housing development. Suzhou Tongfang Alley old city renovation, Changzhou Hongmei Xicun Residential Quarter, Nanjing Longjiang Higher Education Apartment, etc. became the representatives of the residential quarters constructed in that period. Local governments had built a large number of residential quarters under the housing project for those families with housing difficulties. In the mid- and late 1990s, high-rise residential buildings began to appear with the adoption of the country's promoted "new technologies, new processes, new materials, and new equipment" in design and construction, thus the residential quality was further improved. The housing difficulties had been greatly eased.

改造前的桐芳巷
Tongfang Alley before the renovation

苏州桐芳巷住宅小区是全国第一批旧城改造项目，开发、保护、传承并重，彰显了苏州古城历史价值，1996 年获联合国人居范例奖
Suzhou Tongfang Alley Residential Quarter was one of China's first old city renovation projects. It gave equal weight to development, protection and continuity and demonstrated the historical value of Suzhou as an ancient city. Therefore, this quarter was awarded UN-Habitat Scroll of Honor Award by the UN-HABITAT in 1996

常州红梅西村是全国第二批城市住宅小区建设试点项目，获得中国建筑业最高奖——鲁班奖，是90年代中期住宅小区建设的样板

Changzhou Hongmei Xicun was among China's second group of urban residential quarter construction pilot projects and it won the Luban Prize, the highest award in China's construction industry. It was a model residential quarter developed in the mid-1990s.

全国最大的高校教职工安居工程
——南京龙江高教公寓
（龙江花园城阳光广场、月光广场）

The majestic appearance of Nanjing Longjiang Higher Education Apartment (Sunlight Square and Moonlight Square of Longjiang Huayuancheng), China's largest housing project for university teachers and staff members

徐州市科教人员住宅小区——风华园

Fenghuayuan, a residential quarter for the scientific and education staff in Xuzhou

被国家房改办、建设部领导誉为"具有一流水平"的安居工程
——苏州新升新苑小区

Suzhou Xinsheng Xinyuan Residential Quarter, a housing project reputed "at the first-class level" by the leaders of the National Housing System Reform Leading Group Office and the Ministry of Construction

徐州最大的国家安居工程——民富园小区

Minfuyuan Residential Quarter — Xuzhou's largest national housing project for low-income families

南通最大的经济适用住房——北濠东村小区

Beihao Dongcun Residential Quarter — Nantong's largest affordable housing project

住房装修开始走入寻常百姓家，居住品质、舒
适度逐步提高

Housing decoration entered the homes of general
people for rising living standard and comfort

书房　Study room

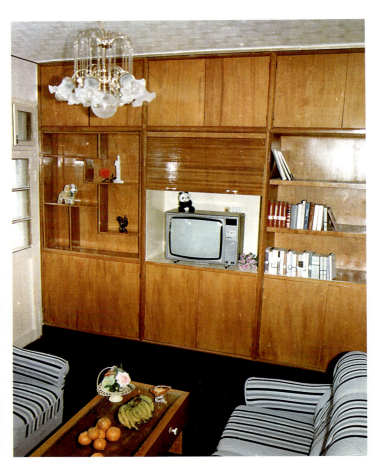

客厅　Living room

厨房　Kitchen

过年聚餐，卧室变成了餐厅
The bedroom acted as a temporary dining-together site in celebration of the New Year

代表性户型图
Representative blueprint

餐厅 Dining room

客厅 Living room

住区配套 Residential district facilities

小区配套幼儿园
Kindergarten in the residential quarter

小区配套游泳池　Swimming pool in the residential quarter

物业管理成为新建小区的标配
Property management became a standard item for a new residential quarter

室内可视对讲监控设备
Indoor visual intercom monitoring equipment

垃圾箱　Garbage can

信报箱　Mail boxes

小区机动车库　Garage of the residential quarter

2000 年以来 —— 温馨家园 | Since 2000 —— Comfortable Homes

　　进入新世纪以来，住房制度改革不断深化，住房公积金制度不断完善，房地产市场快速发展，为住房建设注入强大动力。住宅小区的规划设计、环境和设施配套更加注重"以人为本"，新建住宅小区大量采用新技术、新工艺、新装备、新材料，住房品质进一步提升。商品住房的供给不断满足了老百姓日益增长的住房需求，至2009 年，全省城镇人均住房面积已超过 30 多平方米，为政府做好住房困难家庭保障托底提供了强大的支撑。

Since the entry of the new century, the reform of housing system has continuously deepened, the housing accumulation fund system has constantly improved, and the rapid development of the real estate market has injected powerful impetus to the housing construction. The planning and design, environment and facilities of the residence community pay more attention to the principle of "people first". The new residence communities adopt a large number of new technologies, new processes, new equipment and new materials, which further improve the housing quality. The supply of commercial housing has constantly met people's growing demand for housing. By 2009, the urban housing area per capita of the province had exceeded 30 square meters, providing a strong support for the government to lay the foundation of guarantee for the family with housing difficulties.

无锡市是住房公积金支持保障房建设全国第一批、江苏省第一个试点城市。这组照片为以公积金贷款支持建设的无锡惠景家园保障房实景

Real exteriors of Huijing Jiayuan, a secured housing project built by use of the pubic provident fund loan in Wuxi City, the first pilot city of Jiangsu and one of China's first batch of pilot cities in granting housing provident fund loans for development of secured housing

拆迁安置经济适用住房——南京积善新寓小区

Jishan Xinyu Residential Quarter, Nanjing — a residential quarter of affordable housing for resettlement of households involved in demolition

人才公寓——南通四海家园小区

Apartment for qualified young people, Sihai Jiayuan Residential Quarter, Nantong

全省第一个共有产权住房——淮安福星花园小区

Fuxing Huayuan Residential Quarter, Huai'an — Jiangsu's first housing project with joint property

环境优美、配套齐全的经济适用住房——南京五福家园小区

Wufu Jiayuan, an affordable residential quarter with beautiful environment and complete supporting facilities in Nanjing

由政府设立的专门机构建造的
大型经济适用住房——南京景
明佳园小区

Jingming Jiayuan, a large affordable
residential quarter built by a specialized
agency of Nanjing Municipal Goverment

连云港经济适用住房——茗馨花园小区
Mingxin Huayuan, an affordable residential quarter in Lianyungang

全省第一批国家康居示范工程——南京聚福园小区

Jufuyuan Residential Quarter in Nanjing, one of Jiangsu's first national prosperous housing demonstration projects

国内最高等级 3A 住宅性能认定——南通
中洋高尔夫公寓

Nantong Zhongyang Golf Apartment, a project rated 3A (domestically highest grade) on residential performance

全省第一个采用外墙内保温技术按 65% 建筑节能标准建设的商品住房——徐州滨湖花园小区

Binhu Huayuan in Xuzhou Residential Quarter, Jiangsu's first commodity housing project developed according to the 65% building energy-conversation standard with external wall insulation technology applied

代表性户型图
Representative blueprint

节能省地环保型住宅——苏州枫情水岸小区

Fengqing Shui'an in Suzhou Residential Quarter, an environment-friendly housing project featuring conservation of energy and land

老旧住区改造 Reconstruction of old residential areas

既有住宅小区改造时将"平改坡"与增设地下机动车库一并实施的代表性项目——南京市公教一村小区改造前后对比

Nanjing Gongjiao Yicun Residential Quarter, a typical renovation project implementing "replacement of flat roof with pitched roof" and increasing underground garages (before and after the renovation)

与夫子庙地区建筑风格相协调的既有住宅小区改造代表性项目——南京市武定门北巷小区改造前后对比

Nanjing Wudingmen Beixiang, a typical renovation project of existing residential quarter in harmony with the architectural style of the Confucius Temple area (before and after the renovation)

以违建拆除、设施配套、环境整治、
增加公共活动空间为重点的成片老旧
住区改造典型项目——
南京南湖小区改造前后对比

Nanjing Nanhu Residential Quarter, a typical
renovation project of old residential cluster by
dismantling the illegal buildings and structures,
providing service facilities, improving the
environment and increasing the public space
(before and after renovation)

泰州市既有住宅小区环境整治典型
小区——工人新村改造前后对比

Gongren Xincun, a typical renovation project of
an existing residential quarter in Taizhou City

盐城市既有住宅小区公共改造设施配
套典型项目——毓龙公寓改造前后对比

Yulong Apartment, a typical renovation project
of an existing residential quarter by adding
public facilities in Yancheng City

获得住建部"中国人居环境范例奖"项目
——常州红梅西村河塘前后对比

River of Hongmei Xicun in Changzhou that won "Habitat Scroll of Honor of China" from the Ministry of Housing and Urban-Rural Development

苏州市开展的专项行动——厕所改造，告别马桶

Washroom renovation — saying farewell to chamber pots, a special operation in Suzhou

新娘子、大姑娘少了件烦心事

苏州将"告别"马桶

15年送走6万只，余下4万只8年灭光

有着"人间天堂"美誉的苏州城，今天打响了向最后4万只马桶"宣战"的战役。从1985年起，苏州经过15年的努力，已"消灭"马桶近6万只，而再准备用8年左右时间，彻底与马桶"告别"。

苏州虽历经2500年沧桑，仍保持了"河街相邻、水陆并行"的古城格局和"小桥、流水、人家"的特有风貌。然而，悠久的历史也

久，3个街坊工程全部完成新建住宅30万平方米，70个家庭搬进了独门独户房，"告别"了马桶。3个街人均建筑面积从过去的15方米提升到25.1平方米，粉墙黛瓦，古风犹存。199苏州开始实施第二批街坊

性改造，截至今年10月底，古城区54个街坊已完成改造16个上过去10年动迁总共"消灭"马桶6万只。一些迁入新居的子和大姑娘说，过去最怕的事，是早上起来倒马桶，现有这件烦心事了。

苏州是一座有名的古城，比意大利威尼斯建城早

住区配套 Residential district facilities

门卫　The guard

地下停车库　Underground garage

健身游乐区
Fitness & recreation area

超市
Supermarket

银行
Bank

公交车站　Bus stop

垃圾转运站　Garbage transfer station

进入新世纪后的城市新貌二
The New Look of Cities in the 21st Century II

2010 年以来——住有所居 | Since 2010 — Having Housing to Live in

2010 年以来，江苏以率先实现全面小康为目标，住房建设向更加注重环境质量、更加注重人民生活需求的方向转型发展。一方面着力解决城镇弱势群体的住房困难问题，大力建设保障性住房，推进棚户区、城中村的改造，建立和完善住房保障体系；另一方面着力推进住房绿色发展，打造人与自然和谐共生的居住环境，建成一批综合品质优良、环境优美、和谐宜居、具有引领示范作用的住宅小区。适应人口老龄化社会发展需要，推进适老住区建造。不断推进住宅产业现代化，提升住宅综合品质和性能。到 2017 年，全省城镇居民人均住房面积增长了 8 倍多，基本实现了住有所居。

Since 2010, Jiangsu has taken the lead in achieving the development with the realization of the overall moderate prosperity for the goal, and the transformation of housing construction which pays more attention to environmental quality and people's life needs. On the one hand, Jiangsu has strove to solve the housing difficulties of the urban disadvantaged groups through vigorously building affordable housing, promoting the reconstruction of shanty towns and urban villages, and establishing and improving the housing security system. On the other hand, it has put forth efforts to advance the green housing development and build the living environment with harmony between human and nature, and has built up a group of harmonious and livable residence communities with high comprehensive quality and beautiful environment, as well as the guiding and demonstration effect. In order to adapt to the developmental needs of the aging population society, Jiangshu has been promoting the construction of residential areas suitable for the aged. It has been constantly promoting the modernization of the housing industry and improving the comprehensive quality and performance of housing. By 2017, the urban housing area per capita of the province had increased by more than eight times, basically realizing that everyone has his home to live.

徐矿集团棚户区改造项目——庞庄棚户区改造前后对比

Pangzhuang, a rundown urban area renovation project of Xuzhou Coal Mining Group (before and after renovation)

入住公租房很安心
It is reassuring to live in the public rental housing

小区内锻炼很健康
Taking exercises in the community makes people healthy

小区出行很便捷
The convenient transportation around the community

南京市采用代建模式实施的大型保障房建设项目——南京花岗保障房片区实景
Real exteriors of Nanjing Huagang housing cluster, a large government-subsidized housing project adopting the mode of entrusted construction in Nanjing

环境优美的大型保障房——扬州佳家花园小区　Jiajia Huayuan Residential Quarter, a large and beautiful subsidized housing project in Yangzhou

产业园区为外来人员建设的"优租房"——苏州菁英公寓

Suzhou Elite Apartments — Advanced rental houses for non-locals in an industrial area

苏州菁英公寓入住居民

Residents of Suzhou Elite Appartments

住区内配置养老公寓，实现子女与父母"一碗汤"距离的社区居家养老新模式——南通海门龙馨家园

Nantong Haimen Longxin Jiayuan, a new kind of community equipped with a nursing facility for the aged on the residential ground that provide for a short distance between the children's residence and their elderly parents' home

获得规划设计、建筑设计、施工组织管理、产业化成套技术应用四个单项优秀奖的国家康居示范工程代表——盐城市钱江方洲住宅小区

小区文化

Residential area culture

小区环境

Residential area environment

Qianjiang Fangzhou Residential Quarter in Yancheng, a typical national housing demonstration project that won four excellency awards for planning design, architectural design, construction management and application of industrialized sets of technology

融入古运河文化环境、具有浓郁"扬州味"的商品房——扬州菜茵苑小区

Laiyinyuan Residential Quarter in Yangzhou, a commodity housing project in harmony with the cultural environment of the ancient canal, built in characteristic "Yangzhou style"

全省首个成品住房交付住区——南京金鼎湾国际小区

Fully furnished apartment — Jindingwan Residential Quarter, Nanjing

代表性户型图

Representative blueprint

老旧住区改造 Reconstruction of old residential areas

老旧住宅加装电梯项
目——南京察哈尔路16
号9幢住宅楼加装电梯
前后对比

No. 9 Apartment Building,
No.16 Chahar Road, Nanjing
—Attaching an external
elevator for the old building
(before and after elevator
installation)

苏州彩香新村外露楼
梯安全加固改造前后
对比

External stairs of Caixiang
Xincun Residential Quarter,
Suzhou (before and after
sheltering)

扬州荷花池小区老人食堂

Canteen for senior citizens, Yangzhou
Hehuachi residential quarter

适老住区建设 Construction of the aged-friendly residential areas

商品房社区居家养老项目——扬州市桐园小区

Yangzhou Tongyuan, a commodity housing quarter piloting home-based care for the aged

常州金东方养老住区部分场景

Jindongfang Nursing Area for the aged in Changzhou

住区配套 Residential district facilities

物业服务中心
Property management service center

副食品市场　Non-staple market

地下车库　Underground garage

云柜　Express mail deposit cabinets

入户门禁智能系统　The smart entrance guard system

社区幼儿园 Community kindergarten

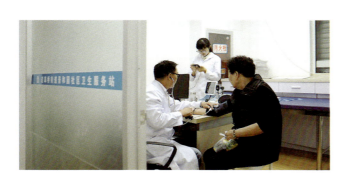

社区卫生服务中心　Community health service center

健身场地与设施　Community Fitness Equipment

第二章 | 实践篇

CHAPTER 2 Practices

解决城镇居民住房问题，是个世界性难题。改革开放之初，江苏如同全国其他省份一样，面临着百废待兴、百业待举的严峻形势。随着城市人口迅速增加，以及大量上山下乡人员返城，住房问题尖锐突出。江苏各级政府和企事业单位，从实际出发，不等不靠，进行了住房制度变革的积极探索，从先行先试，到确立新体制，到稳步推进；从停止住房实物福利分配，到推动住房商品化、货币化；建设模式从单位宿舍楼的零星插建，到住区的综合开发、配套建设，持续不断提升住宅品质和住区环境质量；对部分无力进入住房市场、无力解决自身住房问题的城镇低保和低收入住房困难家庭，政府进行住房保障托底。到"十二五"末，江苏作为全国的缩影，比较好地解决了住房这一世界性的难题，基本圆了江苏城镇居民的住有所居之梦。

The urban housing issue is a world-wide problem. In the early stage of reform and opening-up, Jiangsu, like other regions all over the country, faced the severe situation that all things need to be done. As the fast increasing of urban population, and the people going and working in the countryside and mountainous areas went back to cities, housing problem became more and more serious. Governments at all levels and enterprises and public institutions of Jiangsu got started from reality. They did not depend on others or waited for help, but proactively took effort to carry out the reform of housing system. They carried out the reform according to the following steps: pioneering to practice and pilot, taking new measures, confirming the new system and then pushing forward steadily. The housing mode was changed from stopping the housing distribution welfare system, to the promotion of commercialization and monetization of housing. The old construction mode of the dormitory buildings scattering in units were replaced by a new construction mode. Housing was comprehensively developed with the construction of supporting facilities, and the quality of housing and the quality of residential environment have been continually improving. For the urban residents with minimum social security and low income families, who are incapable of affording houses or no place to live, government offered basic security housing. By the end of "the 12th Five-year Plan" period, Jiangsu, as the epitome of China, had solved the worldwide housing problem well, and basically realized Jiangsu urban residents' dream of having a house to live.

制度变革 | Institutional Reform

　　曾经，福利分房深深地铭刻在人们的脑海中，人们的住房观念是"等、靠、要"。国家和单位"统建、统配、低房租、高补贴"的住房制度难以为继。改革开放之初，邓小平曾指出："解决住房问题能不能路子宽些，譬如允许私人建房，或者私建公助、分期付款，把个人手里的钱动员出来，国家解决材料，这方面的潜力不小。"之后，江苏根据国家的总体要求，开展了深入研究和积极探索。进入90年代后，江苏房改，坚持"迈小步、不停步"，先后推出提租补贴，出售公房，直至全面停止实物分房，迈入住房商品化的新时期。

There was a time when the welfare-oriented public housing distribution system remained etched in people's mind and people's conception of housing was "waiting, relying on and requesting". The country and units' housing system of "unified construction, unified distribution, low rent and high subsidy" became unsustainable. At the beginning of the reform and opening up, Deng Xiaoping pointed out: "The solution to the housing problem should be wider. For example, the private can be allowed to build buildings with installment. The personal money can be mobilized, and the state can solve materials, of which the potential should be great." Hereafter, according to the overall requirements of China, Jiangsu carried out in-depth research and active exploration. Entering the 1990's, in terms of housing reform, adhering to the principle of "small steps without stop", Jiangsu successively launched housing rent subsidies and sales of public housing, until the total cessation of physical housing distribution and the beginning of a new period of commercialization of housing.

1992 年 3 月 6 日《苏州日报》关于苏州市政府按照江苏省政府部署实施住房制度改革的相关报道

On March 6, 1992, *Suzhou Daily* reported that the Suzhou Municipal Government carried out a housing system reform in accordance with Jiangsu Provincial Government's deployment

江苏住房制度改革和住房公积金管理在探索中不断发展完善。1995 年 12 月，苏州市在全国房改经验交流会上作住房公积金归集工作经验介绍

Jiangsu Province's housing system reform and housing provident fund management had been developed and improved in explorations. In December 1995, Suzhou introduced its work experience on collection of housing provident funds at the national housing reform experience exchange meeting

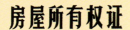

80 年代公有房屋、私有房屋房屋所有权证封面

Front covers of the public housing and private housing title certificates in the 1980s

南京实施公房使用权差价有偿交换

Nanjing implemented the paid exchange of the public housing use rights based on price difference

南京、扬州市公有住房使用费收缴凭证

Payment receipts for the usage of public housing in Nanjing and Yangzhou

直管公房租赁合约

Rental agreement of public housing

先行先试 | Daring to Pilot

1982 年 4 月，常州市被国务院列为补贴出售公有住房改革试点的四个城市之一。

In April,1982, Changzhou was ranked as one of the four cities piloting subsidized sales of public housing by the State Council.

常州市补贴出售住宅改革记事

Changzhou's reform records on subsidized sales of housing

国家首批公有住房补贴出售试点，常州市清潭新村（住房售价每平方米 150 元，政府、单位、个人各出三分之一）

Changzhou acted as one of China's first batch piloting subsidized sales of public housing with the example of Qingtan Xincun Residential Quarter (the housing price was 150 *yuan* per square meter and the government, the work unit and the individual each paid by one third respectively)

1991 年国家和江苏省发布的住房制度改革有
关文件

Documents concerning the housing system reform
promulgated by the State and Jiangsu Province in 1991

1992 年 7 月 1 日，南京市建立住房
公积金制度。到 1995 年年底，全省
所有市县都建立了住房公积金制度。
1996 年国家领导人对苏州市开办个人
住房低息贷款综合保障作出批示

On July 1, 1992, Nanjing pioneered the
establishment of the housing provident fund
system in Jiangsu Province. By the end of 1995,
all cities and counties in Jiangsu Province had
established a housing provident fund system.
In 1996, the state leaders made instructions on
Suzhou's provision of comprehensive security of
low-interest personal housing loans

江苏提出并积极推进住房公积金专户管理、开设个人账户等做法被纳入国务院《住房公积金管理条例》。

Those measures of carrying out special account management and establishing personal accounts of housing provident fund, which were proposed and promoted in Jiangsu,had been listed in Regulations on the Administration of Housing Provident Fund by the State Council.

1993 年 4 月 7 日，原建设银行苏州分行职工钱光达用住房公积金贷款购买了三元三村 46 栋二单元 601 室，建筑面积 65 平方米。该套住房成了我省第一例用住房公积金贷款购买的个人产权住房，钱光达也成为我省用住房公积金贷款购房的第一人

On April 7, 1993, the former employee Qian Guangda of the Construction Bank of China Suzhou Branch used the housing provident fund loan in buying a house property of 46-2-601 of Sanyuansancun Residetial Quarter with a floor area of 65 square meters. This apartment became Jiangsu Province's first private house property bought by use of the housing provident fund loan and Mr. Qian Guangda also became Jiangsu's first person to use the housing provident fund for estate purchase

苏州市住房公积金中心负责人回访我省 1993 年第一例用住房公积金贷款购房的受益家庭

The person in charge of the Suzhou Housing Provident Fund Center visited Jiangsu Province's first family that benefited from the use of the housing provident fund loan for estate purchase in 1993

1994 年苏州第一代住房公积金缴存卡

In 1994, the first-generation housing provident fund depositing cards appeared in Suzhou

1995 年 7 月，泰州市第一笔住房公积金贷款 1.5 万元发放给泰州市招贤中学的教师李藩，用于购买商品房 57.37 平方米

In July 1995, Taizhou City's first housing provident fund loan of 15,000 yuan was granted to Li Pan, a teacher of Taizhou Zhaoxian High School for purchase of a commodity housing of 57.37 square meters

1992 年 8 月 4 日，徐州市民第一笔提取住房公积金的资料

On August 4, 1992, Xuzhou City witnessed the first occurrence of citizen withdrawal of housing provident fund

1998 年，省房改办对常州开设住房公积金个人账户请示的批复

In 1998, Jiangsu Provincial Housing Reform Office gave an official reply to Changzhou's application for establishment of personal accounts of housing provident fund

稳步推进 | Taking Steady Steps

徐州市出售公有住房办理柜台　The sales counter for public housing in Xuzhou

房政简报

第 1 期

江苏省人民政府住房制度改革办公室　1997年2月17日

常熟市全面建立住房公积金
制度，住房公积金余额突破亿元

　　去年7月，常熟市房改办提出了巩固城区、覆盖乡镇，在建制镇（乡镇）全面建立公积金制度的口号。起初乡镇公积金制度的发展很不平衡。针对这种情况，一方面，市房改办的各级领导多次深入各建制镇，宣传动员，做过细的工作，取得了镇领导的支持，提高了基层单位的认识；另一方面，充分发挥了农业银行的作用，市农行在各建制镇网点，确定了公积金协交员，有效地承担了协助催缴公积金的任务；同时，市房改办出台了一系列政策措施，促进公积金制度在各建制镇的全面建立，根据《建制镇职工购建住房贷款办法》，房改办及时向建制镇职工发放政策性住房贷款，使职工群众得到了参加公积金制度的好处。有关政策还规定，凡未参加公积金制度的单位，其职工不得享受房改售房的有关优惠政策。

— 1 —

1998年，淮阴市（现淮安市）成立了全省首家住房贷款担保有限公司，开展住房公积金贷款"一站式"服务

In 1998, Huaiying (today's Huai'an), established the first corporation for offering securities for bank loans, combining all services needed for taking out a loan

无锡市住房公积金综合服务大厅　The combined service hall for housing funds in Wuxi

2011 年，住建部和江苏省进一步加强住房公积金风险防控工作

In 2011, the Ministry of Housing and Urban-Rural Development and Jiangsu Province increased the risk prevention control of housing funds

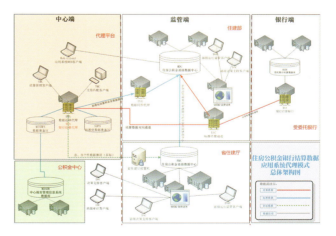

淮安市应用住房公积金银行结算数据系统

The data system for housing fund bank clearings used in Huai'an

确立体制 | Establishing the System

1998年，江苏停止住房实物分配，确立住房商品化、货币化新体制、新机制。

In 1998, Jiangsu put an end to the policy of physical allocation of housing, thus newly establishing commercialization and monetization of housing.

1993年，仪征化纤集团公司率先开展公有住房出售试点

In 1993, the Yizheng Chemical Fiber Company was the first to sell public housing

以张家港港务局为代表的国有企业率先建立住房新体制，开展住房货币化分配试点

State-owned enterprises such as Zhajiagang Port Authority took the lead in establishing a new housing system and piloting the monetized housing distribution

089

市场发展 | Market Development

萌动起步 | Starting up

　　1992 年，江苏房地产市场萌动起步，从公房使用权无偿交换到有偿交换，住房的商品属性开始显现。随着房地产综合开发、配套建设，以及住房金融、物业服务的逐步发展，住房品质与住区环境稳步提升，房地产市场得到了快速发展。

The year 1992 sow the beginning of the real estate market in Jiangsu. With this transformation from voluntary exchange of public housing usage rights to paid exchange houses turned into marketable commodities. As the realty market drove the creation of houses with attached facilities, the housing finance and the property service markets developed, the real estate market grew rapidly.

1992 年 10 月，南京市在全省率先成立房地产市场管理部门

In October 1992, Nanjing took the lead in establishing a real estate market administration sector in Jiangsu Province

1993 年南京市换房大会现场　　The 1993 housing exchange conference

综合开发 | Developing in an All-around Manner

　　在国家法律法规政策指导下，实行"统一规划、配套建设"的房地产综合开发模式，有效地提高了房地产开发效率，不断满足了人们日益增长的住房需求。

　　Under the guidance of the national regulations and policies, a new pattern of comprehensive development of the real estate market, "unified planning and the construction of affiliated facility" was implemented, which improved the efficiency of the real estate development and satisfied the increasing needs of housing.

《中华人民共和国城市房地产管理法》
Law of the People's Republic of China on the Administration of the Urban Real Estate

《城市房地产开发经营管理条例》
"Development and management regulations for unban real estate"

《中华人民共和国物权法》
Property Law of the PRC

房屋买卖契约
House sales contracts

住宅质量保证书、住宅使用说明书
Quality certification of a house, Manual of the house usage

房地产权利证书
The property right certificates

配套服务 | Supporting Services

房产登记服务大厅　Real estate registration service hall

房地产市场金融超市
Real estate market financial
one-stop service supermarket

南 京 市 存 量 房
交 易 合 同
（经纪机构版）

存量房中介交易合同

Nanjing Transaction Contract
of House Property in Stock
(intermediary version)

房地产估价报告
Real estate evaluation report

房产交易会现场　Real estate trade fair

万人看房团活动　Major property tour

置业担保服务窗口
Housing assurance service desk

物业服务　Rendering property services

装饰公司人员和业主沟通
The decoration company personnel talking to a property owner

品质提升 | Improving the Quality

　　建立住宅产业化基地，创建示范工程，开展住宅性能认定，推进住宅产业现代化，提升了住宅综合品质和性能。江苏推动装配式住宅、成品住房、绿色建筑融合发展，住宅产业现代化发展水平领先全国。

By establishing bases of housing industrialization, creating model projects, and the classification of housing, the housing industry is modernizing and high quality is guaranteed. Jiangsu combines the development of fabricated buildings, finished buildings and ecological buildings, and takes the lead in the modernization of the housing industry in China.

住宅部品部件工厂生产预制楼梯、内外墙板、叠合楼板等

Factory production of prefabricated stairs, internal and external wall boards, laminate floor slabs and other building components

整体厨房
Kitchen module

整体卫浴
Bathroom module

南京市丁家庄 A-28 地块全装配、全装修、绿色三星保障性住房

Indemnificatory, 3-star ecological housing with fully equipped ground tiles, fully furnitured, Dingjiazhuang A-28, Nanjing

保障托底 | Government Subsidization

系统化设计 | Systematic Design

2007 年以来，江苏着力推进住房保障体系建设，对住房保障制度进行了系统化设计，在全国率先构建了住房保障体系健全率七项指标，明确了重点任务，制定实施了三年行动计划和十二五规划，持续推进棚户区改造，改善了 800 万住房困难群众的居住条件，为促进社会和谐发展作出了重要贡献。

Since 2007, Jiangsu has pushed forward the construction of housing security system, systematically designed the housing security system, took the lead in building the seven indicators of the housing security system in China, defined the key tasks, formulated and implemented the three-year action plan and the 12th Five-year Plan, continued to promote the reconstruction of shanty towns, and improved the living conditions of 8 million people with housing difficulties, with important contributions to promoting the harmonious development of society.

江苏住房保障体系健全率七项指标	江苏住房保障体系建设七项重点任务
1 新增保障性住房完成率 — Completion rate of increase in affordable housing	1 完善住房保障基本制度 — Improving the basic housing security system
2 住房公积金覆盖率 — Degree of coverage of housing provident fund	2 优化保障性住房建设和供应 — Optimizing the construction and supply of government-subsidized housing
3 住房保障信息化管理达标率 — Compliance rate of housing security information management	3 落实住房保障支持政策 — Implementing the housing security support policy
4 住房保障管理服务网络健全率 — Degree of soundness of housing security management service network	4 健全管理服务网络 — Improving the management service network
5 住房保障制度完善率 — Degree of soundness of housing security system	5 建立投资运营管理机制 — Establishing the investment operation and management mechanism
6 棚户区（危旧房）改造覆盖率 — Degree of coverage of rundown urban area (dilapidated housing) renovation	6 健全保障性住房准入退出机制 — Improving the government-subsidized housing access and withdrawal mechanism
7 城镇保障性住房覆盖率 — Degree of coverage of urban government-subsidized housing	7 实施住房保障信息化管理 — Implementing housing security information management

江苏住房保障体系健全率七项指标
Seven indicators that constitute the "soundness rate of the housing security system"

江苏住房保障体系建设七项重点任务
7 key aspects of housing security in Jiangsu

三年行动计划 | 2008—2010 年
Three-year Action Plan 2008 — 2010

全省新增廉租住房 Number of the low-rent housing in Jiangsu	3.6 万套 36,000 units
新开工建设经济适用住房 Number of new construction of affordable housing	15 万套以上 More than 150,000 units
发放廉租住房租赁补贴 Provision of low-rental housing rental subsidies	4 万户以上 More than 40,000 households
完成重点片区危旧房改造项目 Number of dilapidated housing renovation projects completed in key blocks	684 个 684
改造危旧房建筑面积 Floor area of dilapidated buildings renovated	1651 万平方米 16,510,000 square meters

十二五住房保障规划 | 2011—2015 年
The 12th Five-Year Housing Security Plan 2011—2015

建设保障性安居工程住房 Number of subsidized housing	139 万套（间）廉租住房 1,390,000 units
廉租住房 Number of low-rental housing	2 万套 20,000 units
公共租赁住房 Number of public rental housing	48 万套（间） 480,000 units
经济适用住房 Number of affordable housing	15 万套 150,000 units
完成各类棚户区危旧房改造 Completion of renovation of rundown urban areas and urban dilapidated buildings	3500 万平方米（按每户 50 平方米算，可解决 70 万户家庭的住房困难） by 35,000,000 square meters (if 50 square meters are provided for each family, the completed renovation area is available to help 700,000 families out of housing difficulties).
发放廉租住房租金补贴 Provision of rental subsidies for low-rental housing	4 万户 40,000 households

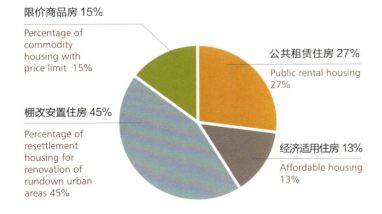

限价商品房 15%
Percentage of commodity housing with price limit 15%

棚改安置住房 45%
Percentage of resettlement housing for renovation of rundown urban areas 45%

公共租赁住房 27%
Public rental housing 27%

经济适用住房 13%
Affordable housing 13%

"十二五"期间新增保障性住房 160 万套（间）
An increase of 1,600,000 subsidized housing units during the 12th Five-Year Plan

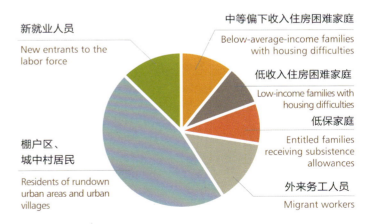

新就业人员
New entrants to the labor force

棚户区、城中村居民
Residents of rundown urban areas and urban villages

中等偏下收入住房困难家庭
Below-average-income families with housing difficulties

低收入住房困难家庭
Low-income families with housing difficulties

低保家庭
Entitled families receiving subsistence allowances

外来务工人员
Migrant workers

"十二五"期间改善约 500 万户居民居住条件
About 5 million residents enjoyed improved housing conditions during the 12th Five-Year Plan

制度化安排 | Institutional Arrangements

　　江苏省人民政府先后制定出台了《省政府关于解决城市低收入家庭住房困难的实施意见》、《省政府关于加快棚户区（危旧房）改造工作的实施意见》，颁布了第50号、51号、73号令，建立了江苏廉租住房、经济适用住房、公共租赁住房等"租售并举"的住房保障制度。

The People's Government of Jiangsu introduced "Suggestions for Solving the Housing Issues of Low-Income Families by the Government of Jiangsu Province", "Suggestions on Accelerating the Renovation of Shanty Towns (Old Dilapidated Housing)", promulgated regulations 50, 51 and 73 and founded the institution of low rent houses, affordable houses, public rental houses and so on.

南京市住房保障服务窗口

Nanjing housing security service window

规范化建设 | Regulated Construction

　　江苏住房保障因城施策，坚持"基本制度统一、实现方式多元"，坚持政府主导、社会参与、市场化运作，采用集中建设、配建、收购、租赁等方式多渠道筹集房源，基本形成了科学合理的保障性住房建设供应体系。

The housing security policy varies in different cities, insisting on "unified institution, various implementations". The government plays the leading role, the society participates and the market operates. The housing source is collected from centralized construction, allocated construction, purchasing, renting and so on; a scientific and reasonable support system for housing security is established.

垃圾生化处理站
Biochemical treatment station for garbage

污水处理系统
Sewage treatment system

和谐邻里　Friendly neighborhood

城中村改造安置用房项目——南京江畔人家小区

Reconstruction of urban villages into resettlement housing project
— Jiangpan Renjia Residential Quarter in Nanjing

长效化推进 | Long-term Promotion

江苏率先实施公共租赁住房和廉租住房并轨运行，完善经济适用住房共有产权模式，因地制宜实施棚改货币化安置、政府购买棚改服务，积极探索"外来务工人员享受新市民同等待遇"、"租售并举"、"阳光担保"。江苏住房保障长效化推进的实践探索和试点经验，得到了国家多次肯定和推广。

Jiangsu was the first to implement both public rental housing and low-rental housing in parallel, to improve the mutual property right housing of affordable housing, to implement the monetized resettlement of renovation of shanty towns and purchase the service of the renovation. Jiangsu actively explores the " equal treatment of migrant workers as new citizens", "rent and sale simultaneously " and "sunlight guarantee". The exploration and experience of the long-term effective housing security of Jiangsu, has been praised and spread throughout the country.

第一批交房现场

The first round of sales

全省住房保障体系建设公廉并轨试点小区——太仓南城雅苑

Nancheng Yayuan, Taichang — A provincial pilot residential quarter integrating public rental housing and low-rental housing for development of the housing security system

2007 年 9 月淮安市第一批共有产权住房发证现场

The site of title certificate issuing for Huai'an first batch of joint property housing units in September 2007

2010 年 3 月，国务院发展研究中心首次提出"淮安共有产权住房保障模式"

The first "Huai'an joint property housing security pattern", proposed by the Development Research Center of the State Council, held in March 2010

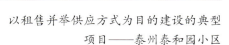

以租售并举供应方式为目的建设的典型项目——泰州泰和园小区

Taizhou Taiheyuan, a typical residential quarter project built for renting and selling

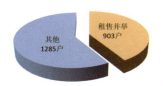

受惠于租售并举政策的群众

People benefiting from the integrated selling and renting policy

截至 2015 年年底，泰州市区经适房保障户数：通过阳光担保获住房保障的户数占 23.4%

By the end of 2015, 23.4% of families owning affordable housing were recipients of a loan granted through the "sunlight guarantee"

截至 2015 年年底，泰州市区经适房保障户数：通过租售并举获住房保障的户数占 41.3%

By the end of 2015, 41.3% of families owning housing affordable through renting and selling

国务院农民工工作联席会议
简　报

2010 年第（13*）期　总第 154 期

国务院农民工工作联席会议办公室　　　2010 年 7 月 7 日

江苏省南通市率先将农民工
纳入市区经济适用住房保障范围

近期，江苏省南通市政府下发《关于将优秀农民工和缴纳社会保险时间较长的外来农民工纳入市区经济适用住房保障范围的试行意见》（简称《意见》），新 8 月初，南通市第一批农民工将能够领到经济适用住房钥匙，这一举措，在江苏省乃至全国开创了农民工享受城市住房保障的先河。

按照分步实施、逐步解决的原则，《意见》规定从 2010 年

— 1 —

2010 年 7 月 7 日，国务院农民工作联席会议简报表彰南通率先将农民工纳入市区经济适用住房保障范围

On July 7, 2010, the Joint Conference of the State Council on Migrant Workers' Work issued a bulletin to commend Nantong's pioneering practice of bringing migrant workers in the urban affordable housing coverage.

"新市民"参加经济适用房摇号

"New citizens" drew lots for access to affordable housing

南通将优秀农民工和缴纳社会保险时间较长的外来农民工纳入市区经济适用住房保障范围，成为享受同等待遇的新南通人

The government of Nantong introduced a model for the inclusion of off-farm workers and migrant workers with long-term paid social insurance into the housing security of urban affordable housing, making them new and equal citizens of Nantong

金明远家庭喜迁宿迁市经济适用住房康堡小区

The Jin Mingyuan family happily moved to Kangbao, an affordable housing quarter in Suqian

受益于棚户区改造的徐州新河花园李广德家庭

The Li Guangde family dwelling in Xuzhou Xinhe Huayuan that has benefited from the renovation of the shanty towns

数说住房 | Housing Figures

2017年，江苏省城镇居民家庭户均拥有住房1.1套，人均住房建筑面积比1978年的4.3平方米增长了8倍多。

In 2017, the per urban household has 1.1 sets of houses in Jiangsu, and the per capita floor space increases over eight times more than the 4.3 square meters in 1978.

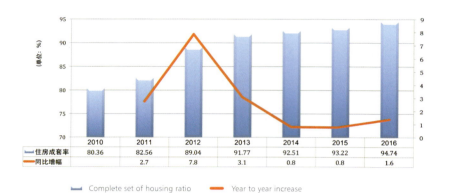

2010 — 2016 年江苏省住房成套率变化情况

Trend of complete set of housing ratio in Jiangsu from 2010 to 2016

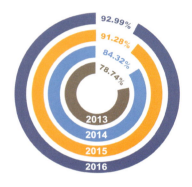

2013 — 2016 年全省住房保障体系健全率

Soundness rate of provincial housing security system from 2013 to 2016

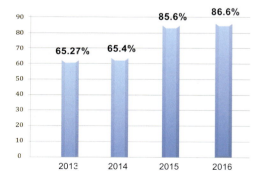

2013 — 2016 年住房满意度调查情况

Satisfaction with the housing situation from 2013 to 2016

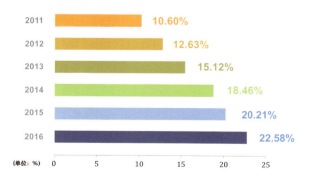

2011 — 2016 年全省城镇保障性住房覆盖率

Degree of coverage of government-subsidized housing in urban areas of Jiangsu from 2011 to 2016

单位：亿元　Unit: 100 million *yuan*

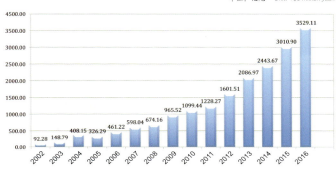

2002－2016 年全省住房公积金贷款余额柱状图

Histogram of balance of the provincial housing provident funds loans
from 2002 to 2016

单位：亿元　Unit: 100 million *yuan*

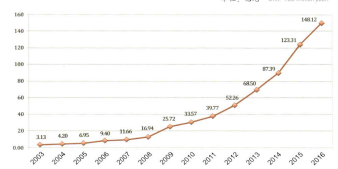

2003－2016 年江苏省住房公积金累计上缴保障房建设补充资金走势图

Trend chart of additional funds accumulatively paid for affordable housing construction of Jiangsu
provincial housing provident funds from 2003 to 2016

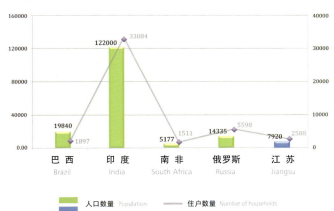

2012 年金砖国家人口数量、住户数量与江苏省的对比

Comparison between BRIC countries and Jiangsu on population and number
of households in 2012

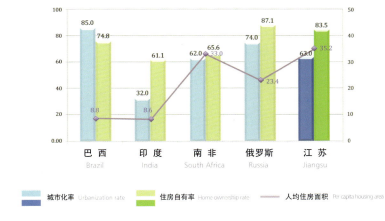

2012 年金砖国家城市化率、住房自有率、人均住房面积与江苏省的对比

Comparison between BRIC Countries and Jiangsu on urbanization rate, home
ownership rate and per capita housing area in 2012

第三章 ｜ 展望篇

CHAPTER 3 Prospects

　　江苏住房在迈向住有宜居的新的历史征程中，着力推进"两聚一高"新实践、建设"强富美高"新江苏发展战略，遵循联合国人居署"人人享有适当住房"、"住房可持续发展"的理念和方针，完善住房保障和供应体系，全面提升住区配套服务水平，注重住房绿色发展，努力让全省城镇居民拥有更加舒适的居住条件。

———————————————————————

　　Jiangsu Housing is stepping into the new era of habitability. We are putting forth effort to promote the new practices of "two focuses and one high level", and the building of new Jiangsu featuring "Strong Economy, Rich People, Beautiful Environment, and High Degree of Social Civilization", following the philosophy and idea of United Nations Human Settlements Program "everyone has access to affordable and adequate housing" and "sustainable development of housing", improving housing security and supply system, comprehensively enhancing the level of supporting services in residential areas, paying attention to the green development of housing, and striving to enable all the urban residents in the province to have more comfortable housing conditions.

住房保障和供应体系更加完善 | The Housing Security System and the Housing Supply System Will Become More Perfect

公租房品质不断提升

The quality of public rental housing constantly improves

人才房筑巢引凤

The social security housing for talents provides good environment

医养结合的养老住宅小区

The residential quarter for the aged with the combination of medical treatment and endowment

下拉式吊柜　Drop-down wall cupboard

无障碍通行坡道

The rampway for barrier-free accessibility

棚户区危旧房改造

Renovation of shanty towns and dilapidated buildings

房屋租赁中介服务　Rental agency

住房信息化　Informatisation of housing market

农民工子弟在城市入学越来越容易

It will become easier for the children of migrant workers to enter schools in cities

住区配套服务水平全面提升

The Supporting Service Level in Residential Areas Comprehensively Upgrades

智慧物业服务 Smart Property Service

智慧物业——"互联网＋物业管理"

Smart Property — "wireless internet and property service"

业主版手机应用 App

Cellphone apps for proprietary

小区监控智能化管理中心 Smart control center within a residential quarter

保安巡查　Security patrol

小区入口服务　Entrance service

快件服务　Express package service

保洁服务　Facility maintenance

维修服务　Maintenance service

安心装修服务 Reassuring Decoration Service

网上报价系统
Online price quotes

消费者体验虚拟装修效果 Consumers experience virtual decoration

手机选材界面
Picking materials with a cell phone interface

装配化装修
Assembly decoration

贴心适老服务   Service for the Elderly

老人食堂   Canteen for seniors

老人体检   Physical check-up for senior citizens

适老设施
Facilities for the aged

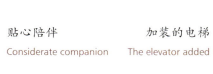

贴心陪伴   加装的电梯
Considerate companion   The elevator added

更加注重住房绿色发展

Paying More Attention to the Green Housing Development

成品化的模块住宅建筑
Construction with fully equipped residence modules

节能窗　Environmentally-friendly window

太阳能屋面　Solar panel roof

屋顶花园
Roof garden

小区绿化　Residential green landscape

地下室采光
Skylight for underground basement

地下车库
Underground garage

住有所居向住有宜居迈进 | The Goal of Having Housing to Live in Changes to Live Comfortably

幸福居住　Living happily

邻里一家亲　A family of neighbours

小区文化活动　Residential area culture activities

青春活力　The vigor of youth

乐在传承　The joys of passing on legacies

安 心 Assured
住房质量有保障
The housing quality is guaranteed

放 心 Safe
安防设施保安全
Security facilities ensure public security

舒 心 Comfortable
居住环境美如画
The living environment is picturesque

省 心 Easy
拎包入住成品房
The finished housing is ready in place

贴 心 Considerate
物业服务到你家
Property management at your service

住房是**家**的载体
Housing is the embodiment of home

家的**安定**和**幸福**是和谐社会的基础
The stability and happiness of families constitute the foundation of a harmonious society

附录 | 江苏住房大事记 1978—2017

Appendix | Jiangsu Housing Milestones (1978—2017)

1978 —1998 年 住房寻找出路阶段

(1978—1998) Pursuit of Housing Development

1978 年 1 月 11 日 中共江苏省委决定恢复设立省基本建设委员会。省建委设城市建设处办理房产住宅行政事务。

January 11, 1978 CPC Jiangsu Provincial Committee decided to resume the establishment of Jiangsu Provincial Capital Construction Committee that governed Urban Construction Department for administration of residential housing.

1978 年 4 月 4 日 中共中央以中发（〔78〕第 13 号）通知印发第三次全国城市工作会议制定的《关于加强城市建设工作的意见》。《意见》提出，目前城市职工住宅严重不足，城市住宅的"缺口"要抓紧补上。

April 4, 1978 The Central Committee of the Communist Party of China issued "Opinions on Strengthening Urban Construction" (Zhong Fa〔78〕No. 13) that was developed in the Third National Urban Work Conference. The "Opinions" required covering the supply gap of urban housing as soon as possible for a serious shortage of housing units for urban staff and workers.

1978 年 9 月 国务院副总理谷牧在全国城市住宅建设会议上传达中共中央副主席邓小平关于解决住房问题的指示："解决住房问题能不能路子宽些，譬如允许私人建房，或者私建公助、分期付款，把个人手里的钱动员出来，国家解决材料，这方面的潜力不小。"

September 1978 At the National Urban Housing Construction Conference, Vice Premier Gu Mu of the State Council conveyed CPC Central Committee Vice Chairman Deng Xiaoping's instructions on solving the housing problem: "It is preferred to increase the channels to solve the housing problem, such as allowing individuals to build houses, or encouraging private construction with public subsidies granted, or paying in installments to encourage individuals to spend money and make the country supply materials. It is of considerable potential."

1978 年 10 月 19 日 国务院批转国家建委《关于加快城市住宅建设的报告》（国发〔1978〕222 号），要求各地区、各部门结合具体情况，参照《报告》中提出的各项措施意见，认真落实投资、资料，尽快把住宅建设的专业队伍建立起来，把住宅建设搞上去，为迅速改变城市住宅的紧张状况而奋斗。

October 19, 1978   The State Council approved and disseminated "Report on Accelerating the Construction of Urban Housing" by the National Construction Committee (Guo Fa〔1978〕No. 222), requiring all regions and sectors to seriously prepare the investment and information in combination with the actuality and with a reference to the measures and suggestions of the Report, organize specialized teams for housing construction and promote the housing construction to facilitate the achievement of the purpose of rapidly easing the shortage of urban housing.

1978 年 10 月 20 日   邓小平副主席视察北京新建的前三门高层住宅建筑时指出：今后修建住宅楼时，设计要力求布局合理，增加使用面积；更多地考虑住户的方便，如尽可能安装一些淋浴设施等；注意内部装修美观，采用新型轻质建筑材料，降低房屋造价。

October 20, 1978   Vice President Deng Xiaoping, when visiting the newly built high-rise buildings in the block of Zhengyangmen, Xuanwumen and Chongwenmen in Beijing, instructed that "In the future construction of residential buildings, the design should strive to achieve reasonable layout to increase the usable area; the convenience of residents should be taken into consideration considerably such as installation of some shower facilities as much as possible; attention should be paid to the esthetic appearance of interior decoration and new type of lightweight building materials should be applied to reduce the cost of housing.

1980 年 3 月 2 — 11 日   国家城市建设总局召开的全国城市住宅工作会议提出，要加快城市住宅建设，力争做到新账不再欠，老账积极还，以逐步改善城市人民的住房状况；要鼓励私人建房；要采取多种形式组织私人购房。

March 2—11, 1980   At the National Urban Housing Working Conference, the State Administration of Urban Construction proposed to speed up the construction of urban housing and strive to achieve no delay of new construction and supplementation of construction in arrears so as to improve the urban people's housing status in successive steps, encourage individuals to build houses; and adopt a wide range of means to organize individuals to buy houses.

1980 年 4 月 15 日   中共江苏省委决定成立江苏省城镇建设局主管城市建设行政工作。内设住宅房产处。

April 15, 1980   CPC Jiangsu Provincial Committee decided to establish Jiangsu Provincial Urban Construction Bureau for administration of urban construction. Under the Bureau was Residential Housing Department.

1981年9月　江苏第一家房地产开发企业——中国房地产开发常州总公司成立。

September 1981　Jiangsu's first real estate development enterprise — China Real Estate Development Changzhou Corporation was incorporated.

1982年4月17日　《国务院关于城市出售住宅试点问题的复函》（〔82〕国函字60号）确定常州市被国务院列为补贴出售公有住房改革试点的四个城市之一。常州市按"出售公房，提高房租"的改革思路实行补贴出售公有住房改革试点。1983—1985年，共出售新建住房1478套，计8.2万平方米。建设部副部长刘志峰在《江苏房改》所作的前言中指出："常州市是1982年4月国务院'三三制'售房的试点城市，为制定和完善公有住房出售政策起到了重要作用。"

April 17, 1982　It was decided in "Reply of the State Council on Piloting Sales of House Properties in Urban Areas" (〔82〕Guo Han Zi No. 60) that Changzhou was chosen by the State Council as one of the four cities piloting the reform on subsidized sales of public housing. Changzhou piloted the public housing reform by subsidized sales according to the reform idea of "selling the public housing and raising the rental". A total of 1,478 newly-built housing units with total area of 82,000 square meters were sold from 1983 to 1985.Vice Minister of the Ministry of Construction Liu Zhifeng pointed out in the foreword of the book *Jiangsu Housing Reform* that "Changzhou was chosen to pilot the execution of '1/3-1/3-1/3 system' for housing sales by the State Council in April 1982 and it had played a vital role in developing and improving the public housing sales policy."

1982年10月9日　江苏省人大常委会第16次会议原则批准《江苏省城市建设用地管理和房屋拆迁安置试行办法》，江苏省人民政府于同年11月18日公布施行。

October 9, 1982　"Proposed Regulations of Jiangsu Province on Urban Construction Land Management, Housing Demolition, Relocation and Resettlement" was approved in principle at the 16th Session of Jiangsu Provincial People's Congress Standing Committee and it was promulgated for implementation by Jiangsu Provincial People's Government on November 18 of the same year.

1983年2月21日　江苏省城镇建设局印发《关于"文革"期间挤占私房和私房改造若干具体问题的处理意见》。

February 21, 1983　Jiangsu Provincial Urban Construction Bureau released "Opinions on Handling Issues Concerning Occupation of Private Houses and Reconstruction of Private Houses in the 'Cultural Revolution' Period".

1983年4月17日　国务院批准同意江苏省省级党政机构改革方案，确定省基本建设委员会和省城镇建设局合并，组建江苏省建设厅。翌年2月10日，经国务院批准，省建设厅改称江苏省建设委员会。内设房产管理处。

April 17, 1983　The State Council approved Jiangsu's provincial party and government institutional reform program, determining the establishment of Jiangsu Provincial Department of Construction by combining Jiangsu Provincial Capital Construction Committee and Jiangsu Provincial Urban Construction Bureau. On February 10 of the next year, Jiangsu Provincial Department of Construction was renamed Jiangsu Provincial Construction Committee upon the approval of the State Council. Under it was Housing Office.

1983年5月25日　国务院批准《城镇个人建造住宅管理办法》（〔83〕国函字109号）。同年6月4日，城乡建设环境保护部发施行（〔83〕城住字第367号）。《办法》规定，城镇居民或职工可以建造私人住宅，按正式户平均，一般每人不得超过20平方米。可以民建公助，也可以自筹自建或互助互建，房权归个人所有。

May 25, 1983　The State Council gave an official reply "Administrative Regulations on Individual Construction of Houses in Urban Areas" (〔83〕Guo Han Zi No. 109). The Ministry of Urban and Rural Construction and Environmental Protection issued the document of (〔83〕Cheng Zhu Zi No. 367) on June 4. It was provided in the "Regulations" that urban dwellers or workers were permitted to construct private houses and generally the per capita area should not exceed 20 square meters on average for official households. It was permitted for individuals to build with the public assistance, or raise funds to build by oneself or cooperate with others for building, and the houses built in these means would be owned by the individuals.

1983年12月15日　国务院发布《国务院关于严格控制城镇住宅标准的规定》（国发〔1983〕193号）。规定全国城镇和各工矿区住宅均应以中小型户（一至二居室一套）为主，平均建筑面积应控制在50平方米以内。

December 15, 1983   The State Council issued "Regulations of the State Council on Strict Control over Urban Residence Standard" (Guo Fa〔1983〕No. 193). It was provided that the housing of the cities and towns, industrial and mining areas throughout the country shall be dominated by medium and small-sized apartments (a suite with one or two bedrooms) and shall be controlled not more than 50 square meters per suite averagely on the floor area.

1983 年 12 月 17 日   国务院发布《城市私有房屋管理条例》(国发〔1983〕194 号)，对城市私有房屋的所有权登记、买卖、租赁、代管和适用范围等，作了具体规定。

December 17, 1983   The State Council promulgated "Administrative Regulations on Urban Private Housing" (Guo Fa〔1983〕No. 194) to give particulars on proprietorship registration, trade, leasing, escrow and applicability of private housing in urban areas.

1984 年 7 月 5 日   城乡建设环境保护部、国家统计局经国务院批准，发出《关于开展全国城镇房屋普查的通知》(〔84〕城住字 391 号)，附发《第一次全国城镇房屋普查办法》，确定以 1985 年 6 月 30 日为这次普查的标准时间。普查工作由城乡建设环境保护部和国家统计局共同组织，以城市、县城（镇）和独立工矿区范围内的全部房屋为对象，采取统一普查办法，查清全国城镇房屋的数量、质量，以及占有、使用、居住等基本情况。同年 10 月 24 日，江苏省人民政府办公厅发出《关于开展城镇房屋普查的通知》（苏政办发〔1984〕68 号)，确定具体普查业务由市县房管部门或城乡建设局负责，统计部门给予协助。

July 5, 1984   The Ministry of Urban and Rural Construction and Environmental Protection and the National Bureau of Statistics issued "Notice on Carrying out General Investigation of House Properties in Urban Areas of China" (〔84〕Cheng Zhu Zi No. 391) attached with "Regulations on the First National General Investigation of Urban Housing", determining the date of June 30, 1985 as the standard time for the current investigation. The general investigation was jointly organized by the Ministry of Urban and Rural Construction and Environmental Protection and the National Bureau of Statistics. Taking all house properties within the ranges of cities, counties (towns) and independent industrial and mining areas, the general investigation was aimed at investigating and ascertaining the quantity and quality of urban house properties throughout China and the possession, use, dwelling and other basic information through unified investigation methods. Jiangsu Provincial People's Government Office issued "Notice on Carrying out General Investigation of Urban Housing" (Su Zheng Ban Fa〔1984〕No. 68) on October 24 of the same year, determining that the specific investigation task shall be completed by the municipal/county housing administration authority or the urban and rural construction bureau and assisted by the statistical sectors.

1984 年 10 月 11 日　　国务院批转城乡建设环境保护部《关于扩大城市公有住宅补贴出售试点的报告》（国发〔1984〕140 号）。11 月 8 日，城乡建设环境保护部印发《关于扩大城市公有住宅补贴出售试点工作的通知》（〔84〕城住字第 665 号）。《通知》指出：公有住宅补贴出售给个人，是逐步推行住宅商品化、全面改革我国现行住房制度的重要步骤，也是当前城市改革的组成部分。

October 11, 1984　　The State Council approved and disseminated "Report on Expanding the Pilot Range of Subsidized Sales of Urban Public Housing" that was submitted by the Ministry of Urban and Rural Construction and Environmental Protection (Guo Fa〔1984〕No. 140). On November 8, the Ministry of Urban and Rural Construction and Environmental Protection distributed Notice on Expanding the Pilot Range of Subsidized Sales of Urban Public Housing" (〔84〕Cheng Zhu Zi No. 665). The "Notice provides that: Selling public housing to individuals with subsidies granted is an important step for pushing forward housing commoditization progressively and reforming China's prevailing housing system in all aspects and it is also part of the current urban reform.

1986 年 4 月 15 日　　江苏省建设委员会、江苏省物价局联合下发《关于改革城镇非住宅公房租金的意见》，揭开了城镇非住宅公有房屋租金改革的序幕。

April 15, 1986　　Jiangsu Provincial Construction Committee and Jiangsu Provincial Price Bureau jointly issued "Opinions on Reforming the Rental of Urban Non-Residential Public Housing", which marked the debut of the reform on the rentals of urban non-residential public housing.

1986 年 6 月 11 日　　江苏省人民政府颁发《江苏省城镇房地产管理暂行办法》，同时废止 1954 年江苏省人民委员会公布的《江苏省公有房地产管理暂行办法》。

June 11, 1986　　Jiangsu Provincial People's Government promulgated "Interim Measures of Jiangsu Province on Real Estate in Urban Areas" and abolished "Interim Measures of Jiangsu Province on Public Real Estate" that was promulgated by Jiangsu Provincial People's Committee in 1954.

1987年4月　　国务院第一次提出"土地使用权可以有偿转让"的政策，并在天津、上海、广州、深圳开展国有土地使用权有偿有限期转让改革试点。1987年12月1日，深圳率先敲响了拍卖国有土地使用权的第一槌，突破了土地使用权不允许转让的法律规定。

April 1987　　The State Council proposed the policy that " the land use right may be transferred with pay" for the first time and initiated the pilot work of paid transfer of the state land use right for a fixed term in Tianjin, Shanghai, Guangzhou and Shenzhen. On December 1, 1987, Shenzhen took the lead in launching the public sale of the state land use right, which was a breakthrough of the statutory provision prohibiting land use right transfer.

1987年8月19日　　江苏省建设委员会下发《关于开展城镇房屋所有权登记、发证工作的通知》。

August 19, 1987　　Jiangsu Provincial Construction Committee issued "Notice on Implementation of Urban Housing Proprietorship Registration and Certificate Distribution".

1987年12月21日　　江苏省人民政府决定成立江苏省住房制度改革领导小组。领导小组办公室设在省建设委员会。

December 21, 1987　　Jiangsu Provincial People's Government decided to establish Jiangsu Housing System Reform Leading Group. The office of the Leading Group was located in Jiangsu Provincial Construction Committee.

1988年1月15日　　国务院召开第一次全国住房制度改革工作会议。

January 15, 1988　　The State Council convened the first national housing system reform working conference.

1988年2月25日　　国务院印发《关于在全国城镇分期分批推行住房制度改革的实施方案》（国发〔1988〕11号），决定从1988年起，用三五年的时间，在全国城镇分期分批把住房制度改革推开。

February 25, 1988　　The State Council distributed "Executive Plan on Carrying out Housing System Reform in Cities and Towns Countrywide by Group at Different Times" (Guo Fa〔1988〕No. 11), determining to spend three to five years starting from 1998 in executing the housing system reform in urban areas throughout the country group after group at different times.

1988年3月6日至9日　　江苏省人民政府召开全省住房制度改革工作会议，传达全国房改工作会议精神，对全省房改工作提出"全面部署，分批出台，交叉准备，三年推开"的总要求。

March 6—9, 1988　　Jiangsu Provincial People's Government held a provincial housing reform working conference to convey the spirit of the national housing reform conference and put forward the requirements of "full deployment, introduction in batch, cross-preparation and popularization in three years".

1988年4月12日　　中华人民共和国第七届全国人民代表大会第一次会议通过《宪法修正案》，规定"土地使用权可以依照法律的规定转让"。

April 12, 1988　　It is provided that "the land use right may be transferred in accordance with the law" in the Amendment to the Constitution that was adopted at the First Session of the Seventh National People's Congress of the People's Republic of China.

1988年5月26日　　江苏省人民政府办公厅转发省房改领导小组《关于鼓励职工购买公有旧住房的实施意见》。

May 26, 1988　　Jiangsu Provincial People's Government Office disseminated "Opinions for Implementation of Encouraging Staff Members and Workers to Purchase Old Public Housing" of the Provincial Housing Reform Leading Group.

1988年9月6日　　江苏省人民政府办公厅转发省建委、省侨办、省财政厅《关于落实华侨私房政策中若干具体问题的处理意见》（苏政办发〔1988〕113号）。

September 6, 1988　　Jiangsu Provincial People's Government disseminated "Opinions on Handling Specific Issues Concerning Implementation of the Policy on Private Housing of Overseas Chinese" that was jointly issued by Jiangsu Provincial Construction Committee, Jiangsu Provincial Overseas Chinese Affairs Office, and Jiangsu Provincial Department of Finance (Su Zheng Ban Fa〔1988〕No. 113).

1988年12月7日　　省房改试点城市《南通市市区出售公有住房暂行办法》出台实施。

December 7, 1988   The provincial housing reform pilot city Nantong promulgated "Interim Measures of Nantong City on Sales of Public Housing in Urban Areas".

1989 年 1 月 16 日   省房改试点县《大丰县城镇住房制度改革试行方案》出台，其中售房试点方案开始实施。

January 16, 1989   The provincial housing reform pilot county Dafeng promulgated "Proposal of Dafeng County for Trial Implementation of Urban Housing System Reform", of which the pilot scheme of housing sales was put into operation.

1990 年 2 月 1 日   江苏省土地管理局、江苏省物价局、江苏省财政厅联合印发《江苏省农村非农业建设用地有偿使用收费管理试行办法》（苏土综〔1990〕29 号）。

February 1, 1990   Jiangsu Provincial Land Administration Bureau, Jiangsu Provincial Price Bureau and Jiangsu Provincial Department of Finance jointly issued "Proposed Regulations on Charging the Use of Non-Agricultural Construction Land in Rural Areas of Jiangsu" (Su Tu Zong〔1990〕No. 29).

1990 年 5 月 19 日   国务院发布《中华人民共和国城镇国有土地使用权出让和转让暂行条例》（国务院令第 55 号），对城镇国有土地使用权的出让、转让、出租、抵押做了系统规定，其中居住用地使用权最高年限为 70 年。

May 19, 1990   The State Council promulgated "Provisional Regulations of the People's Republic of China on Assignment and Transfer of Use Rights of State Land in Urban Areas" (State Council Decree No. 55) that systematically stipulated the assignment, transfer, lease and mortgage of state land use rights including the use term of residential land of 70 years.

1990 年 9 月 4 日   建设部发出《关于在全国开展住宅小区管理试点工作的通知》（〔90〕建房字第 450 号），对试点的范围、依据与目标、组织和进度等提出了具体要求。

September 4, 1990   The Ministry of Construction issued "Notice on Implementation of Pilot Management of Residential Quarters Countrywide" (〔90〕Jian Fang Zi No. 450) that covered the specific requirements on the pilot range, basis and objectives, organization and progress.

1990年12月4日　江苏省建设委员会、江苏省总工会转发建设部、全国总工会关于《解决城镇居住特别困难户住房问题的若干意见》（苏建房秦〔1990〕第451号）。

December 4, 1990　Jiangsu Provincial Construction Committee and All-Jiangsu Federation of Labor Unions disseminated "Opinions on Settlement of Housing Difficulties of Extreme Poor Urban Households" by the Ministry of Construction and All-China Federation of Trade Unions (Su Jian Fang Qin〔1990〕No. 451).

1990年12月19日　江苏省第七届人大常委会第18次会议通过并公布实施《江苏省城市房屋拆迁管理条例》，同时废止1982年10月6日江苏省第五届人大常委会第16次会议原则批准的《江苏省城市建设用地管理和房屋拆迁安置试行办法》。

December 19, 1990　"Administrative Regulations of Jiangsu Province on Urban Housing Demolition and Relocation" was approved and promulgated and "Proposed Regulations of Jiangsu Province on Urban Construction Land Management, Housing Demolition, Relocation and Resettlement" that was approved in principle at the 16th Session of the Fifth People's Congress Standing Committee of Jiangsu Province on October 9, 1982 was revoked at the 18th Session of the Seventh People's Congress Standing Committee of Jiangsu.

1990年12月31日　建设部令发布《城市房屋产权产籍管理暂行办法》（建设部令第7号），自1991年1月1日起施行。《暂行办法》共五章二十五条，对城市房屋产权产籍的定义、管理主体、城市房屋产权的管理、城市房屋产籍的管理以及罚则做了规定。

December 31, 1990　The Ministry of Construction promulgated "Interim Measures on Administration of Ownership and Cadastre of Urban Housing" (Ministry of Construction Decree No. 7), which shall be implemented since January 1, 1991. "Interim Measures" consists of 25 articles in five chapters to provide the definitions of ownership and cadastre of urban housing, main body of management, administration of urban housing ownership, management of urban housing cadastre, and penalty provisions.

1991年10月5日　国务院住房制度改革领导小组批准江苏省房改方案《江苏省城镇住房制度改

革实施意见》。同年 11 月 14 日，江苏省人民政府印发《江苏省城镇住房制度改革实施意见》。11 月 20 日至 22 日，省政府在南京召开全省房改工作会议予以贯彻落实，确定"实现住房商品化"的目标和"走小步，不停步，不走回头路"的改革原则，提出"租、售、建并举，以提租为重点，多提少补或小步提租不补贴的租金改革"方案。

October 5, 1991　The State Council Housing Reform Leading Group approved Jiangsu's housing reform proposal "Opinions of Jiangsu Province on Implementation of Urban Housing System Reform". Jiangsu Provincial Government distributed "Opinions of Jiangsu Province on Implementation of Urban Housing System Reform" on November 14. During November 20 to 22, Jiangsu Provincial Government held in Nanjing a provincial housing reform working conference for implementation of the said policy, determining the goal of "realizing housing commoditization" and the reform principles of "taking small steps with no stop or retracing of own steps", and proposing the scheme of "giving equal weight to renting, selling and building, focusing on raising the rent, raising more rent with less subsidy granted or increasing the rent slightly with no subsidy granted".

1991 年 11 月 15 日　江苏省住房制度改革领导小组、江苏省建设委员会印发《江苏省优惠出售公有住房的暂行规定》。

November 15, 1991　Jiangsu Housing System Reform Leading Group and Jiangsu Provincial Construction Committee issued "Provisional Regulations of Jiangsu Province on Preferential Sale of Public Housing".

1991 年 11 月 23 日　国务院发布《关于全面推进城镇住房制度改革的意见》（国办发〔1991〕30 号），明确规范了房改的分阶段及总目标、基本原则、有关政策、工作部署、工作领导等。明确提出城镇住房制度改革的总目标是：按照社会主义有计划商品经济的要求，从改革公房低租金制度着手，将现行公房的实物福利分配制度逐步转变为货币工资分配制度。

November 23, 1991　The State Council issued "Opinions on Promoting the Reform of Urban Housing System in an All-round Way" (Guo Ban Fa〔1991〕No. 30), which clearly specifies the phased and overall goals, basic principles, relevant policies, work arrangements and work leadership of the housing reform. The overall goal of urban housing reform clearly put forward was: Make the existing system of public housing distribution as welfare in kind gradually transformed into the money wage distribution system, starting from the reform of the public housing low rent system in accordance with the requirements of the socialist planned commodity economy.

1991年12月4日　江苏省编制委员会批准同时增挂江苏省建设委员会房地产综合开发管理办公室的牌子，省建委房产管理处更名为房地产业处。

December 4, 1991　Jiangsu Provincial Commission of Public Sectors Reform approved that the tag of Jiangsu Provincial Construction Committee Real Estate Comprehensive Development Management Office was added and Provincial Construction Committee Housing Administration Office was renamed Real Estate Industry Office.

1992年6月　常州市房管局和工商银行常州分行筹资建立了"常州物业公司"，开始从事物业管理工作。

June 1992　Changzhou Municipal Housing Administration Bureau and Industrial and Commercial Bank of China Changzhou Branch raised funds in establishing "Changzhou Property Management Company" to render property management services.

1992年6月17日　江苏省人民政府第118次常务会议决定全省设区的市市区住房制度改革联动起步，要求抓紧制定县（市）实施意见（建立住房公积金，分步提租发补贴，新租公房交定金，职工买房给优惠，实行住房基金制）。同年7月1日，全省11个设区的市市区联动起步实施房改方案，其中，南通市和常州市是1992年6月1日开始实行住房公积金制度。江苏为全国第一个同时全面启动房改实施方案的省份。

June 17, 1992　It was decided at the 118th Executive Meeting of Jiangsu Provincial People's Government to jointly launch the urban housing system reform in all cities divided into districts in Jiangsu, requiring development of county/municipal implementation opinions as soon as possible (including establishment of the housing provident fund, raising the rent with subsidies granted step by step, paying the earnest money for newly leased public housing, granting preferential treatment for staff purchase of house property, carrying out the housing fund system). On July 1 of the same year, 11 cities divided into districts in Jiangsu Province simultaneously started implementation of the housing reform program. Nantong and Changzhou began to implement the housing provident fund system on June 1, 1992. Jiangsu was China's first province in implementing the housing reform scheme in an all-around manner.

1992年7月20日　江苏省人民政府下发《关于省住房制度改革工作机构》的通知，将江苏省住房制度改革领导小组办公室更名为江苏省人民政府住房制度改革办公室。

July 20, 1992　Jiangsu Provincial People's Government issued a notice "On Provincial Housing System Reform Operation Organ" to change the name of Jiangsu Provincial Housing System Reform Leading Group to be the Housing System Reform Office of the People's Government.

1992年下半年　省本级和各设区的市陆续成立住房基金管理中心，负责本级住房基金的归集、管理和使用，为独立法人事业单位，实行独立核算，分别隶属于同级政府行政事务管理局和房产、建设、财政等政府职能部门管理。

Second half of 1992　Housing fund management centers had been established at the provincial level or the cities with districts established, taking charge of the collection, management and use of the housing fund of own level; it, as an independent legal institution, carried out independent accounting and was subject to the administration of the administration bureau, real estate, construction, finance and other functional sectors of the government at the same level.

1992年11月　"中外合资常州天安物业管理分公司"成立，负责常州城北开发区天安工业村的管理，开展对工业厂房的物业管理。

November 1992　"Sino-Foreign Joint Venture Changzhou Tian'an Property Management Branch" was established, in charge of the property management of industrial premises of Tian'an Gongye Village in the development area in northern Changzhou.

1992年11月15日　江苏省人民政府办公厅印发《江苏省县(市)住房制度改革实施意见》。

November 15, 1992　Jiangsu Provincial People's Government Office distributed "Implementation Opinions of Jiangsu Province on County (Municipal) Housing System Reform".

1992年12月18日　江苏省物价局、江苏省建设委员会联合下发《关于深化改革城镇直管非住宅公房租金的通知》（苏价涉字〔1992〕第 232 号）。

December 18, 1992　　Jiangsu Provincial Price Bureau and Jiangsu Provincial Construction Committee jointly issued "Notice on Deepening Reform of Urban Directly-Controlled Non-Residential Public Housing Rental" (Su Jia She Zi〔1992〕No. 232).

1993 年 2 月 11 日至 13 日　　江苏省住房制度改革领导小组在盐城市召开全省经济适用住房建设现场会。

February 11—13, 1993　　Jiangsu Provincial Housing Reform Leading Group held a provincial affordable housing construction site meeting in Yancheng.

1993 年 4 月 1 日　　苏州市首创综合保险担保方式，同年 4 月 7 日在全省率先发放职工个人购、建住房低息贷款。

April 1, 1993　　Suzhou pioneered in providing the mode of comprehensive insurance guarantee and it took the lead in granting employees low-interest loans for individual purchase or building of house properties in Jiangsu on April 7 of the same year.

1993 年 11 月　　全国第三次房改工作会议召开，改变第二次房改会议确定的思路，提出"以出售公房为重点，售、租、建并举"的新方案。

November 1993　　The third national housing reform working conference was held to overthrow the idea determined at the second national housing reform working conference and propose the new concept of "giving priority to sales of public housing and giving equal weight to selling, renting and building of housing".

1994 年 3 月 23 日　　建设部颁发《城市新建住宅小区管理办法》（建设部 33 号令），规定住宅小区产权人、使用人通过选举成立管理委员会，逐步推进社会化、专业化的管理模式。

March 23, 1994　　The Ministry of Construction promulgated "Administration Measures on Urban Newly Developed Residential Quarters" (Decree No. 33 of the Ministry of Construction), which clearly defines that the housing property owners and users of the residential quarters in China establish management committees through election so as to promote the management pattern of socialization and specialization gradually.

1994年7月5日　　中华人民共和国第29号主席令公布《中华人民共和国城市房地产管理法》，自1995年1月1日施行。2007年8月30日，由全国人大常委会第29次会议通过修订，以中华人民共和国第72号主席令公布。

July 5, 1994　　Order No. 29 of the President of the People's Republic of China promulgated the Urban Real Estate Administration Law of the People's Republic of China, which has been effective as of July 1, 1995. On August 30, 2007, the law was amended by the 29th NPC Standing Committee of the People's Republic of China, and promulgated by Order No. 72 of the President of the People's Republic of China.

1994年7月18日　　《国务院关于深化城镇住房制度改革的决定》（国发〔1994〕43号）出台，其核心内容是：建立与社会主义市场经济体制相适应的新的城镇住房制度，实现住房商品化、社会化；把各单位建设、分配、维修、管理住房的体制改变为社会化、专业化运行的体制；把住房实物福利分配的方式改变为以按劳分配为主的货币工资分配方式；建立以中低收入家庭为对象、具有社会保障性质的经济适用住房供应体系和以高收入家庭为对象的商品房供应体系；同时，建立住房公积金制度，建立政策性和商业性并存的住房信贷体系。这在中国城镇住房制度改革历程上具有里程碑的作用，是第一个体现了社会主义市场经济体制要求的改革方案。

July 18, 1994　　"Determination of the State Council on Deepening the Urban Housing System Reform" (Guo Fa〔1994〕No. 43) with the core contents as below: Establish a new urban housing system to adapt to the socialist market economy system to achieve housing commercialization and socialization; change the housing construction, distribution, maintenance, and management system of each unit to be socialized and specialized operation system; change the way of housing distribution in kind as welfare to be the way of distribution in money wages mainly based on distribution according to work; establish an affordable housing supply system that mainly addresses the middle- and low-income families and has the nature of social security and establish a commercial housing supply system to cater to the demands of high-income families; and establish a housing provident fund system and a housing credit system with both the nature of policy and the nature of commerciality. This policy played a milestone role in China's urban housing system reform history as it was the first reform program to reflect the socialist market economy system.

1994年8月13日　　建设部下发《关于贯彻（城市房地产管理法）若干意见》，江苏省建委于1994年9月29日转发至各市、县。

August 13, 1994   The Ministry of Construction issued "Opinions on the Implementation of 'the Law of on the Administration of the Real Estate in Urban Areas'" and Jiangsu Provincial Construction Committee disseminated the said "Opinions" to all cities and counties in Jiangsu on September 29, 1994.

1995 年 1 月   江苏省选择 100 家大中型企业进行住房货币化分配试点。

January 1995   Jiangsu selected 100 middle- and large-sized enterprises to pilot the monetized housing distribution.

1995 年 2 月 6 日   国务院办公厅《转发国务院住房制度改革领导小组国家安居工程实施方案》（国办发〔1995〕6 号）。

February 6, 1995   The General Office of the State Council issued "Notice on Forwarding the Implementation Plan of the National Housing Project of the State Council Housing System Reform Leading Group" (Guo Ban Fa〔1995〕No. 6).

1995 年 2 月 16 日   国务院住房制度改革领导小组召开部署国家安居工程工作电话会议，标志着国家安居工程正式启动实施。

February 16, 1995   The State Council Housing System Reform Leading Group held a teleconference on deployment of the national housing project, marking the official launch of the national housing project.

1995 年 3 月 20 日   江苏省人民政府印发《关于深化城镇住房制度改革的方案》（苏政发〔1995〕29 号），规定"住房公积金经营净收益免征所得税，并专项用于住房建设"。住房公积金增值收益在提取贷款风险准备金和管理费用后，全部用于廉租住房和公共租赁住房建设。

March 20, 1995   Jiangsu Provincial People's Government issued "Plan on Deepening the Urban Housing System Reform" (Su Zheng Fa〔1995〕No. 29), which provides that "the net income from operation of the housing provident fund is exempted from income tax and is used specially for housing development". The incremental benefit of the housing provident fund minus the provision of the loan risk reserve fund and the overhead costs is totally used for the construction of low-rental housing and public rental housing.

1995 年 4 月　南京金銮大厦置业有限公司成立，接管的金銮大厦成为江苏第一个实施物业管理的大厦。

April 1995　Nanjing Jinluan Mansion Real Estate Co., Ltd. was incorporated and its customer Jinluan Mansion thus became Jiangsu's first estate with property management services available.

1995 年 5 月 9 日　建设部第 42 号令公布《城市房屋租赁管理办法》自 1995 年 6 月 1 日起施行。

May 9, 1995　The Ministry of Construction promulgated its Decree No. 42 "Administration Measures on Renting of Housing in Urban Areas" that shall be implemented since June 1, 1995.

1995 年 5 月 11 日至 12 日　江苏省人民政府在南京召开全省房改工作会议，贯彻落实《关于深化城镇住房制度改革方案》。同年 5 月底前，省房改办在南京先后举办了三期全省房改骨干业务培训班。

May 11—12, 1995　Jiangsu Provincial People's Government convened a provincial housing reform working conference for execution of "Plan on Deepening the Urban Housing System Reform". Before the end of May of the same year, the Provincial Housing Reform Office had held in Nanjing three sessions of training courses for the provincial housing reform backbones.

1995 年 8 月 7 日　建设部第 45 号令公布《城市房地产转让管理规定》自 1995 年 9 月 1 日起施行。

August 7, 1995　The Ministry of Construction promulgated its Decree No. 45 "Administration Regulations on Transfer of Urban Estate" that shall be implemented since September 1, 1995.

1995 年 10 月 13 日　江苏省建设委员会出台《江苏省物业管理规定》。

October 13, 1995　Jiangsu Provincial Construction Committee promulgated "Regulations of Jiangsu Province on Property Management".

1995 年 11 月　南京市花园路小区成为省内首批"全国城市物业管理优秀小区"。

November 1995　　Nanjing Huayuanlu Residential Quarter became Jiangsu's first "national excellent urban residential quarter on property management".

1995 年 12 月 15 日　　江苏省住房制度改革领导小组组长刘坚向国务院副总理朱镕基汇报江苏住房基金社会化管理原则的五句话"中心负责，银行办理，财政监督，税务支持，房委会或房改领导小组决策"得到肯定。

December 15, 1995　　Jiangsu Provincial Housing Reform Leading Group Leader Liu Jian reported the housing fund socialization management principle of Jiangsu to Vice Premier Zhu Rongji: The "Center is responsible for the matter, the banking sector proceeds to handle it, the financial authorities exercise supervision and the taxation authorities grant supports, and the housing committee or the housing reform leading group makes a decision", and such principle was acknowledged.

1996 年 9 月 5 日　　江苏省建设委员会下发《关于印发城市房屋拆迁管理"三个办法"的通知》（苏建房〔1996〕447 号），出台了《江苏省城市房屋拆迁实施单位资质管理审查办法（试行）》、《江苏省城市房屋拆迁管理工作考核办法》、《江苏省拆房施工单位资质管理暂行办法》，对房屋拆迁单位资质、拆迁管理工作考核、房屋拆除管理做出了具体明确的规定和要求。

September 5, 1996　　Jiangsu Provincial Construction Committee issued "Notice on Printing and Distribution of 'Three Measures'for Urban Housing Demolition and Relocation Administration (Su Jian Fang〔1996〕No. 447), promulgated "Measures of Jiangsu Province for Management and Review of the Qualifications of Urban Housing Demolition and Relocation Implementation Organizations (Trial Implementation)", "Measures of Jiangsu Province on Assessment of Urban Housing Demolition and Relocation Administration", "Interim Measures of Jiangsu Province for Administration of the Qualifications of Demolition Organizations" to give specific provisions and requirements on the qualifications of the housing demolition and relocation organizations, assessment of demolition and relocation administration, and administration of housing demolition.

1996 年 12 月 23 日　　南京市人民政府发布《南京市物业管理暂行办法》。

December 23, 1996　　Nanjing Municipal People's Government issued "Interim Measures of Nanjing on Property Management".

1997 年 9 月 4 日　　江苏省人民政府在常州溧阳、金坛市召开全省物业管理工作现场会，推动全省物业管理稳步快速发展。

September 4, 1997　　Jiangsu Provincial Government convened provincial property management working conferences on the sites in Liyang and Jintan cities of Changzhou in an effort to promote the provincial property management to develop in a steady and sound manner.

1998 年　　住宅专项维修资金制度建立，南京等地陆续建立物业管理办公室（中心），承担住宅专项维修资金的归集、核算、使用管理等。

1998　　The special residential maintenance fund system was established; Nanjing and other cities had established respective property management office (center) in succession responsible for collection, accounting and use control of the special residential maintenance fund.

1998 年　　江阴、常熟、南通进行住房二级市场交易试点。

1998　　Jiangyin, Changshu and Nantong piloted in secondary housing market trade.

1998 年 3 月 30 日　　省内最先实施廉租住房制度的城市《金坛市人民政府关于廉租住房建设管理暂行办法》（坛政发〔1999〕40 号）出台，该市 1997 年开工建设的 50 套廉租住房于 1998 年分配入住。

March 30, 1998　　"Interim Procedures of Jintan Municipal People's Government on Administration of Low-Rental Housing Construction" (Tan Zheng Fa〔1999〕No. 40) was released in Jintan City which acted as Jiangsu Province's first city in implementing the low-rental housing system. The 50 low-rental housing units that Jintan City started construction in 1997 were put into use in 1998.

1998 年 5 月 12 日　　建设部印发《关于印发〈商品住宅实行住宅质量保证书和住宅使用说明书制度的规定〉的通知》（建房〔1998〕102 号），同年江苏省建设委员会转发此通知，自 1998 年 9 月 1 日起，住宅质量保证书和住宅使用说明书制度在江苏省实施。

May 12, 1998   The Ministry of Construction issued "Notice on Printing and Distribution of 'Regulations on Implementation of the System of Housing Warranty and Housing Operation Instructions for Commodity Housing'" (Jian Fang〔1998〕No. 102) and in the same year Jiangsu Provincial Construction Committee disseminated this notice; and the system of housing warranty and housing operation instructions has been implemented since September 1, 1998.

1998年5月至9月   江苏省建设委员会根据建设部的统一部署和要求，委托东南大学、苏州城建环保学院、南京市房管局教育中心共组织培训部门经理和管理员、物业管理企业经理1763名，受到建设部的表彰。

May to September, 1998   In accordance with the unified deployment and requirements of the Ministry of Construction, Jiangsu Provincial Construction Committee entrusted Southeast University, Suzhou College of Urban Construction and Environmental Protection and Nanjing City Housing Administration Bureau Education Center to organize trainings for 1,763 department heads and administrators, and property management enterprise managers, and such training activities were commended by the Ministry of Construction.

1998年7月20日   国务院第248号令《城市房地产开发经营管理条例》公布施行。2011年1月8日，国务院第138次常务会议审议修订，以国务院第588号令公布施行。

July 20, 1998   The State Council promulgated its Decree No. 248 "Administration Regulations on Development and Operation of Real Estate in Urban Areas". It was deliberated and revised at the 138th Executive Meeting of the State Council and it was promulgated in the Decree No. 588 of the State Council on January 8, 2011.

1998年9月4日   江苏省人民政府第12次常务会议审议通过《江苏省城市住宅区物业管理办法》。同年9月21日以江苏省人民政府第141号令发布施行。

September 4, 1998   "Regulations of Jiangsu Province on Administration of Property Management for Urban Residential Areas" was deliberated and approved at the 12th Executive Meeting of Jiangsu Provincial People's Government. And it was promulgated in the Decree No. 141 of Jiangsu Provincial People's Government on September 21, 1998.

1998年9月24日   江苏省人民政府批转《省住房制度改革领导小组关于进一步深化城镇住房制

度改革的实施方案的通知》（苏政发〔1998〕89号），要求全面停止实物分房。提出对不同收入家庭实行不同的住房供应政策：最低收入家庭可租住政府提供的廉租住房；中低收入家庭购买经济适用住房和普通居民住宅。

September 24, 1998　Jiangsu Provincial Government approved and disseminated "Notice of Provincial Housing System Reform Leading Group on Executive Plan for Further Deepening Urban Housing System Reform" (Su Zheng Fa〔1998〕No. 89), requiring stop of housing distribution in kind in all-round manner. It was put forward that different housing supply policies were provided for different income families. The lowest income families could rent the government's supplied low-rental housing; middle- and low-income families could purchase affordable housing and general residential properties.

1998 年 8 月 26 日　江苏省人民政府印发《关于大力发展住宅建设培育新的经济增长点的若干意见》（苏政发〔1998〕74号）。

August 26, 1998　Jiangsu Provincial People's Government printed and distributed "Opinions on Vigorously Developing Housing Construction to Cultivate New Economic Growth Points" (Su Zheng Fa〔1998〕No. 74).

1998 年 11 月　南京等部分城市开始陆续成立物业管理行业协会。

November 1998　Nanjing and some other cities began to set up property management industry associations in succession.

1999—2007 年　住房市场快速发展阶段
(1999—2007) Rapid Development of Housing Market

1999 年 3 月　江苏省建设委员会、江苏省公安厅联合印发《江苏省城市居民住宅安全防范设施建设管理实施细则》（苏建房〔1999〕106号），进一步规范全省城市住宅区安防设施建设管理行为。

March 1999　Jiangsu Provincial Construction Committee and Jiangsu Provincial Department of Public Security jointly issued "Enforcement Rules of Jiangsu Province on Administration of Construction of Urban Residential Building Safety Prevention and Control Facilities" (Su Jian Fang〔1999〕No. 106) to further regulate the management of the construction of safety prevention and control facilities for residential areas throughout the province.

1999 年 4 月 1 日　建设部印发《国家康居示范工程实施大纲》（建住房〔1999〕98 号）。

April 1, 1999　The Ministry of Construction issued "Implementation Outline of National Comfortable Housing Demonstration Project" (Jian Zhu Fang〔1999〕No. 98).

1999 年 4 月 3 日　国务院颁布第 262 号令《住房公积金管理条例》。标志着我国住房公积金制度进入了法制化、规范化发展的新时期。江苏开设个人账户、专户管理等做法被该《条例》吸收采纳。2002 年 3 月 24 日国务院予以审议修订，以国务院第 350 号令发布施行。

April 3, 1999　The State Council promulgated its Decree No. 262 "Regulations on Management of Housing Provident Fund". It marked that China's housing provident fund system entered a new era subject to the control of statutory provisions. Jiangsu's practices of opening personal accounts and carrying out special account management were adopted in the "Regulations". It was deliberated and revised by the State Council on March 24, 2002 and it was promulgated in the Decree No. 350 of the State Council.

1999 年 8 月 20 日　国务院办公厅转发建设部等部门《关于推进住宅产业现代化提高住宅质量的若干意见》（国办发〔1999〕72 号）。该《意见》为推进我国住宅产业现代化的纲领性文件，明确规定了实施住宅产业现代化战略的指导思想、主要目标、工作重点和相关要求。

August 20, 1999　The General Office of the State Council disseminated "Opinions on Promoting Modernization of the Residential Housing Industry to Improve Housing Quality" that was prepared by the Ministry of Construction and other authorities (Guo Ban Fa〔1999〕No. 72). The "Opinions" became a programmatic document to promote the modernization of China's housing industry. The document clearly stipulates the guiding ideology, main goals, priorities and related requirements for China's implementation of the modernization strategy for the housing industry.

1999 — 2000 年　《江苏省住宅区物业管理服务标准（试行）》（苏建房〔1999〕521 号）、《江

苏省住宅区物业管理服务等级评定标准（试行）》（苏建房〔2000〕75号）、《江苏省普通住宅区物业管理公共服务费等级收费暂行办法》（苏价房〔1999〕500号）先后出台，在全国率先提出了对物业管理服务进行等级评定并确定相应服务费等级的办法。

1999-2000　"Jiangsu Provincial Housing Property Management Service Standard for Residential Areas (Trial Implementation)" (Su Jian Fang〔1999〕No. 521), "Jiangsu Provincial Property Management Service Rating Standard for Residential Areas (Trial Implementation)" (Su Jian Fang〔2000〕No. 75), "Interim Measures of Jiangsu Province on Property Management Public Service Rating and Charging for General Residential Areas"(Su Jia Fang〔1999〕No. 500) had been promulgated in succession. Jiangsu was the first to propose rating property management services and determining the corresponding service charge level.

1999年12月5日　南京百家湖花园住宅区就物业管理单位进行了招投标。

December 5, 1999　Nanjing Baijia Lake Garden Residential Quarter invited to bid for recruitment of a property management service provider.

2000年1月5日　江苏省建设委员会印发《江苏省城市住宅区业主委员会管理办法》（苏建房〔2000〕2号），规范业主委员会的运作和业主的行为，以发挥业主委员会在物业管理中的自治自律作用。

January 5, 2000　Jiangsu Provincial Construction Committee issued "Administration Measures of Jiangsu Province on Urban Residential Area Owners' Committees" (Su Jian Fang〔2000〕No. 2), regulating the operations of the owners' committees and the acts of the owners and making owners' committees play a role of self-rule and self-discipline in property management.

2000年3月20日　南京市龙江小区10幢高教公寓以招标方式面向社会选聘"管家"。爱涛物业和江鸿物业两家物业管理公司分别取得了龙江高教公寓南北两大片区的管理权。

March 20, 2000　The ten high-rise buildings of Nanjing Longjiang Higher Education Apartment recruited "property management service provider" by means of inviting to bid. Aitao Property Management Company and Jianghong Property Management Company were awarded the right to manage the southern/northern blocks of Longjiang Higher Education

Apartment respectively.

2000 年 4 月 27 日　　江苏省建设委员会印发《江苏省物业管理招标投标试行办法》。

April 27, 2000　　Jiangsu Provincial Construction Committee issued "Proposed Regulations of Jiangsu Province on Bidding and Tendering for Property Management".

2000 年 12 月 7 日　　建设部印发《国家康居示范工程管理办法》（建住房〔2000〕274 号），以住宅小区为载体，以推进住宅产业现代化为总体目标，通过示范小区引路，推广应用住宅新技术、新工艺、新产品、新设备，提高住宅综合品质和住宅建设水平。

December 7, 2000　　The Ministry of Construction distributed "Administration Regulations of National Comfortable Housing Demonstration Project" (Jian Zhu Fang〔2000〕No. 274) to take residential quarters as the carriers, take the promotion of the modernization of the housing industry as the overall goal, resort to demonstration quarters to guide and popularize the application of new technologies, new processes, new products and new devices of housing to improve the comprehensive quality and the construction capability of residential buildings.

2000 年 12 月 24 日　　江苏省九届人大常务会第 20 次会议审议通过《江苏省物业管理条例》，并分别于 2003 年 10 月 25 日江苏省第十届人大常委会第 6 次会议、2012 年 11 月 29 日江苏省第十一届人大常委会第 31 次会议进行修订。

December 24, 2000　　Jiangsu Province, the 20th session of the Ninth Standing Committee of Jiangsu Provincial People's Congress adopted the "Regulations on Management in Jiangsu Province", which was amended respectively in the sixth session of the Tenth Standing Committee of Jiangsu Provincial People's Congress on October 25, 2003 and in the the 31st session of the 11th Standing Committee of Jiangsu Provincial People's Congress on November 29, 2012.

2001 年 7 月　　江苏省建设委员会房地产综合开发管理办公室更名为江苏省建设厅住宅产业化促进中心，负责推进全省住宅产业领域的技术进步和现代化工作。

July 2001   Jiangsu Provincial Construction Committee Real Estate Comprehensive Development Management Office changed its name to be Jiangsu Provincial Department of Construction Housing Industrialization Promotion Center, responsible for promoting the technological progress and modernization of the provincial housing industry.

2001年12月5日   江苏省建设厅编制印发《江苏省城市房屋拆迁补偿价评估技术导则（试行）》（苏建房〔2001〕393号）。

December 5, 2001   Jiangsu Provincial Department of Construction edited and distributed "Technical Guidelines of Jiangsu Province on Evaluation of Compensation for Removal due to Urban Housing Demolition (Trial Implementation)" (Su Jian Fang〔2001〕No. 393).

2002年2月5日   江苏省第九届人民代表大会常务委员会第28次会议审议通过《江苏省城市房地产交易管理条例》，2004年8月20日修正。

February 5, 2002   "Administration Regulations of Jiangsu Province on Urban Real Estate Trade" was deliberated and approved at the 28th session of the Ninth Standing Committee of Jiangsu Provincial People's Congress and it was amended on August 20, 2004.

2002年10月23日   江苏省第九届人民代表大会常务委员会第32次会议审议通过《江苏省城市房屋拆迁管理条例》。明确"货币补偿金额，根据被拆迁房屋的区位、用途、建筑面积等因素，以房地产市场估价确定"；实行产权调换的，要结算被拆迁房屋的补偿金额和所调换房屋价格的差价。

October 23, 2002   "Administration Regulations of Jiangsu Province on Urban Housing Demolition and Relocation" was deliberated and approved at the 32nd Session of the Ninth Standing Committee of Jiangsu Provincial People's Congress. It is clearly provided in the "Regulations" that "the monetary compensation amount is determined according to the real estate market valuation in consideration of the factors including location, usage, floor area of the house property under demolition"; if property rights are exchanged, it is required to settle the difference between the compensation amount of the house under demolition and the price of the replacement house.

2003年3月28日 地方标准DB32/T538—2002《江苏省住宅物业管理服务标准》，经国家质量监督检验检疫总局备案（备案号：13209-2003），江苏省质量技术监督局发布实施。

March 28, 2003　The local standard DB32/T538—2002 "Jiangsu Provincial Residential Property Management Service Standard" was filed with the General Administration of Quality Supervision, Inspection and Quarantine (file number: 13209-2003) and it was promulgated for implementation by Jiangsu Provincial Administration of Quality and Technical Supervision.

2003年5月13日 江苏省建设厅印发《江苏省新建住宅全装修试点工作实施意见》（苏建房〔2003〕138号），推行全装修住宅的发展。

May 13, 2003　Jiangsu Provincial Department of Construction distributed "Implementation Opinions of Jiangsu Province on Piloting Full Decoration of Newly Built Residential Buildings" (Su Jian Fang〔2003〕No. 138) to push forward the development of fully-decorated residential buildings.

2003年8月12日 国务院下发《国务院关于促进房地产市场持续健康发展的通知》（国发〔2003〕18号），要求各地建立完善廉租住房制度，把经济适用住房定位于具有保障性质的政策性商品住房。要把住房公积金制度的建设作为深化住房分配制度改革、促进房地产市场持续健康发展的重要内容。

August 12, 2003　The State Council issued "Notice of the State Council on Promoting the Real Estate Market to Develop in a Sustainable and Healthy Manner" (Guo Fa〔2003〕No. 18), requiring all localities to establish and improve the low-rental housing system and position the affordable housing as a policy-oriented commodity housing with the government's support. And it also required taking the construction of the housing provident fund system as an important item to deepen the reform in the housing distribution system and promoting the real estate market to develop in a sustainable and healthy manner.

2003年11月 江苏所有设区城市均设立了住房公积金管委会，并制定了管委会章程，健全了议事规则和决策程序，形成了民主决策、科学决策和自主决策的管理机制。

November 2003　All cities with districts in Jiangsu had set up respective housing provident fund management committee

and developed the rules of association of the management committee to specify the rules of procedure and the decision-making process and form the management mechanism of democratic, scientific and independent decision-making.

2005年5月9日 国务院办公厅转发建设部等部门《关于做好稳定住房价格工作的意见》（国办发〔2005〕26号），《意见》以抑制商品住房价格过快上涨为主要目标，提出以税收等经济手段调节房地产市场。首次明确享受优惠政策的住房原则上应同时满足以下条件：住宅小区建筑容积率在 1.0 以上、单套建筑面积在 120 平方米以下、实际成交价格低于同级别土地上住房平均交易价格 1.2 倍以下。

May 9, 2005 The General Office of the State Council disseminated "Opinions on Effectively Stabilizing Housing Prices" (Guo Ban Fa〔2005〕No. 26) that was jointly promulgated by the Ministry of Construction and others to take the main goal of keeping the price of Commercial Housing from rising too quickly and propose to use economic means such as taxes to adjust the real estate market. For the first time, it clearly defined that the housing enjoy the preferential policy shall in principle meet the following conditions simultaneously: The residential quarter building volume rate is 1.0 or more, the floor area per unit is less than 120 square meters, the transaction price in real terms is lower than the 1.2 times of the average transaction price of the house properties on the same level of land.

2005年5月17日 江苏省人民政府办公厅转发省建设厅、省发展改革委、省财政厅、省国土资源厅、人行南京分行、省物价局、省地税局、江苏银监局《关于切实稳定住房价格促进房地产业健康发展的意见》（苏政办发〔2005〕55号）。

May 17, 2005 Jiangsu Provincial People's Government Office disseminated "Opinions on Effectively Stabilizing Housing Prices to Promote the Healthy Development of the Real Estate Industry" (Su Zheng Ban Fa〔2005〕No. 55) which was jointly promulgated by the Provincial Department of Construction, the Provincial Development and Reform Commission, the Provincial Department of Finance, the Provincial Department of Land and Resources, the Nanjing Branch of the People's Bank, the Provincial Price Bureau, the Provincial Local Taxation Bureau, and China Banking Regulatory Commission Jiangsu Office.

2005年9月 全省房地产市场月报数据和监测报告上报制度建立。

September 2005 The system to reporting the provincial real estate market monthly report data and monitoring reports was established.

2005年11月30日　　国家标准《住宅性能评定技术标准》（GB/T 50362-2005）发布，于2006年3月1日实施。该标准适合所有城镇新建住宅和改建住宅，反映住宅的综合性能水平，体现节能节地节水节材等产业技术政策，倡导土建装修一体化，提高工程质量，引导住宅开发和住房理性消费，鼓励开发企业提高住宅性能。

November 30, 2005　　The national standard "Technical standard for performance assessment of residential buildings"(GB/T 50362-2005) was issued and should be implemented since March 1, 2006. This standard applied to all newly built and rebuilt residential buildings in the urban areas; it reflected residential building's comprehensive properties, embodies the industrial technical policies on saving energy, land, water and materials, advocated the integration of civil work and decoration to improve the quality of construction, guided the development of residential buildings and reasonable consumption of housing, and encouraged real estate developers to improve the residential performance.

2005年12月　　《江苏省志·房地产管理志》出版。

December 2005　　*Annals of Jiangsu Province Records of Real Estate Administration* was published.

2006年5月5—7日　　2006中国（江苏）首届住宅产业国际博览会在南京国际展览中心隆重举行。

May 5—7, 2006　　2006 China (Jiangsu) the First International Exhibition of Housing Industry was held at Nanjing International Exhibition Center.

2006年6月3日　　江苏省建设厅转发建设部《房地产机构管理办法》（苏建房〔2006〕127号），对房地产估价机构和分支机构设立、分支机构设立条件、分支机构不得出具房地产估价报告的行为等进行了规定。

June 3, 2006　　Jiangsu Provincial Department of Construction disseminated "Administration Regulations on Real Estate Organizations"

which was promulgated by the Ministry of Construction (Su Jian Fang〔2006〕No. 127) and the "Regulations" provided the setup of real estate appraisal organizations and their branches, setup conditions of branches, forbidding branches to issue real estate appraisal reports.

2006 年 6 月 21 日　　　建设部印发《国家住宅产业化基地试行办法》（建住房〔2006〕150 号）。

June 21, 2006　　　The Ministry of Construction distributed "Proposed Regulations on National Housing Industrialization Bases" (Jian Zhu Fang〔2006〕No. 150).

2006 年 7 月 25 日　　　江苏省政府办公厅出台《省政府办公厅关于转发国办发〔2006〕37 号文件的通知》（苏政办发〔2006〕99 号），以调整住房供应结构、稳定住房价格为主要目标，提出 90/70 政策等。

July 25, 2006　　　Jiangsu Provincial Government Office issued "Notice of Jiangsu Provincial Government on Forwarding Guo Ban Fa〔2006〕No. 37 Document" (Su Zheng Ban Fa〔2006〕No. 99) to make clear the main objectives of adjusting the housing supply structure and stabilizing housing prices and to put forward the 90/70 policy, etc.

2006 年 9 月 13 日　　　为加强房地产业发展和房地产市场调控指导工作，省政府办公厅印发《省政府办公厅关于建立房地产业发展与房地产市场调控联席会议的通知》（苏政办发〔2006〕114 号）建立省房地产业发展与房地产市场调控联席会议，确定组成人员名单，同时明确联席会议办公室设在省建设厅，承担日常工作。

September 13, 2006　　　In order to strengthen the guidance for the development of the real estate industry and the regulation of the real estate market, Jiangsu Provincial Government Office issued "Notice of Jiangsu Provincial Government Office on Establishment of Joint Conference on Real Estate Industry Development and Real Estate Market Regulation" (Su Zheng Ban Fa〔2006〕No. 114) to determine the establishment of the provincial joint conference on real estate industry development and real estate market regulation, determine the members and indicate that the joint reference office is in Jiangsu Provincial Department of Construction and it is responsible for the routine work.

2006 年 9 月 20 日　　　扬州市荣获联合国人居署颁发的 2006 年度"联合国人居奖"。

September 20, 2006   Yangzhou City won the "UN Habitat Scroll of Honor Award" for year 2006 from UN-HABITAT.

2007 年 3 月 16 日   《中华人民共和国物权法》由第十届全国人大第五次会议通过，以中华人民共和国第 62 号主席令公布，自 2007 年 10 月 1 日起施行。

March 16, 2007   "The Property Law of People's Republic of China" was adopted by the fifth plenary session of the Tenth Standing Committee of the National People's Congress, was promulgated by Order No. 62 of the President of the People's Republic of China, and effective as of October 1, 2007.

2007 年 6 月 11 日   江苏省建设厅出台《江苏省共有产权经济适用房试点办法》（苏建房改〔2007〕197 文号）。淮安、泰州、姜堰等地开展试点。同年 9 月淮安市开展经济适用住房共有产权试点，明确用出让土地建设供应的"共有产权住房"替代划拨土地建设供应的经济适用住房。

June 11, 2007   Jiangsu Provincial Department of Construction issued "Measures of Jiangsu Province on Piloting Affordable Housing with Shared Ownership" (Su Jian Fang Gai〔2007〕No. 197). Huai'an, Taizhou and Jiangyan piloted in this respect. Huai'an City piloted the affordable housing with shared ownership in September 2007 by clearly specifying that the "housing with shared ownership" constructed on the land acquired through transfer replaced the affordable housing constructed on the land acquired through allotment.

2007 年 6 月 12 日   南京栖霞建设集团通过论证，成为江苏省第一家国家住宅产业化基地。

June 12, 2007   Nanjing Qixia Construction Group succeeded in passing the argumentation to become Jiangsu's first national base for housing industrialization.

2007 年 8 月 7 日   国务院出台《关于解决城市低收入家庭住房困难的若干意见》（国发〔2007〕24 号）。

August 7, 2007   The State Council issued "Opinions on Solving the Housing Difficulties of Low-Income Families in Urban Areas" (Guo Fa〔2007〕No. 24).

2007 年 8 月 24 日—25 日　全国城市住房工作会议在北京召开。

August 24—25, 2007　　The national urban housing working conference was held in Beijing.

2007 年 12 月 4 日　建设部发布《住宅专项维修资金管理办法》（建设部令第 165 号），自 2008 年 2 月 1 日起施行。

December 4, 2007　　The Ministry of Construction promulgated "Administration Regulations on Special Housing Maintenance Funds" (Ministry of Construction Decree No. 165), which should be implemented since February 1, 2008.

2007 年 12 月 4 日　全省城市住房工作会议在南京召开，会议就解决城市低收入家庭住房困难工作进行了部署。

December 4, 2007　　The provincial urban housing working conference was held in Nanjing to arrange the settlement of the housing difficulties of the low-income families in the urban areas.

2007 年底　全省市、县（市、区）全部建立廉租住房制度，提前一年达到国家对东部地区规定要求。

End of 2007　　The low-rental housing system was established in all cities and counties (districts) of Jiangsu, marking the completion of the country task one year ahead of schedule.

2008 年至今　基本实现住有所居阶段

From 2008 up to now, it is the stage for Jiangsu to basically achieve that everyone has a house to live

2008 年 5 月 5 日　《省政府关于解决城市低收入家庭住房困难的实施意见》（苏政发〔2008〕44 号），提出，省政府决定成立省城市住房与房地产工作领导小组，负责研究提出解决城市低收入家庭住房困难的有关政策，完善城市住房制度和政策体系，调控房地产市场以促进房地产发展，协调解决工作实施中的重大问题。领导小组办公室设在省建设厅，负责日常工作。

May 5, 2008   "Implementation Opinions of Jiangsu Provincial Government on Solving the Housing Difficulties of Urban Low-income Families"(Su Zheng Fa〔2008〕No. 44) proposed that Jiangsu Provincial Government decided to establish the Provincial Urban Housing and Real Estate Work Leading Group to be responsible for research and proposal of policies on solving the housing difficulties of urban low-income families, improvement of the urban housing system and policy system, regulation and control of the real estate market to promote the real estate development, and coordination in settlement of grave issues appearing in the practice. The Provincial Urban Housing and Real Estate Work Leading Group works in Jiangsu Provincial Department of Construction, responsible for routine work.

2008 年 7 月 21 日   《中共江苏省委江苏省人民政府关于切实加强民生工作若干问题的决定》（苏发〔2008〕14 号）出台，要求为争用 3—5 年时间，使群众关注的突出民生问题得到较好解决。要建立健全以廉租房制度为重点、多渠道解决住房困难问题的住房政策体系，切实改善低收入家庭和其他困难群体的居住条件。

July 21, 2008   "Decision of CPC Jiangsu Provincial Committee and Jiangsu Province People's Government on Issues Concerning Effective Improvement of the People's Wellbeing" (Su Fa〔2008〕No. 14) was issued, requiring to spend three to five years in basically solving major wellbeing concerns of the people. Establish and improve the housing policy system that gives priority to low-rental housing and relying on multiple channels to solve the housing difficulties, thus improving the housing conditions of low-income families and other people with difficulty effectively.

2008 年 10 月 6 日   联合国人居署宣布颁发南京市联合国人居奖特别荣誉奖。

October 6, 2008   UN-HABITAT announced to award Special UN Habitat Scroll of Honor Award to Nanjing.

2008 年 11 月 3 — 6 日   第四届世界城市论坛在南京举行，以"和谐的城镇化"为论坛主题。中国住房和城乡建设部与联合国人居署共同主办，中国公安部、国家环境保护部和江苏省人民政府协办。

November 3—6, 2008   The Fourth World Urban Forum was held in Nanjing with the topic of "harmonious urbanization".

It was sponsored by the Ministry of Housing and Urban-Rural Development of the People's Republic of China and the UN-HABITAT and it was co-sponsored by the Ministry of Public Security, the Ministry of Environmental Protection and Jiangsu Provincial People's Government.

2008 年 11 月　　建立全省房地产市场交易信息动态周报制度。

November 2008　　The weekly report system of the provincial real estate market transaction information was established.

2008 年 12 月 3 日　　《江苏省廉租住房保障办法》（省政府令第 50 号）和《江苏省经济适用住房管理办法》（省政府令第 51 号）发布，自 2009 年 1 月 1 日起施行。

December 3, 2008　　"Measures of Jiangsu Province on Provision of Low-Rental Housing" (Decree No. 50 of Jiangsu Provincial Government) and "Measures of Jiangsu Province on Administration of Affordable Housing" (Decree No. 51 of Jiangsu Provincial Government) were promulgated and they should be implemented since January 1, 2009.

2008 年 12 月 9 日　　江苏省制定发布《全省住房保障三年行动计划（2008—2010）》（苏政发〔2008〕131 号），提出通过 3 年时间建设廉租住房 3.6 万套，经济适用住房 15 万套，发放廉租住房租赁补贴 12 万户，完成危旧房改造 1651 万平方米。

December 9, 2008　　Jiangsu Province developed and issued "Jiangsu Provincial Housing Security Three-Year Action Plan (2008—2010) (Su Zheng Fa〔2008〕No. 131), proposing to spend three years in construction of 36,000 low-rental housing units, 150,000 affordable housing units, distribution of low-rental housing subsidies to 120,000 families and completion of renovation of dilapidated housing of 16,510,000 square meters.

2008 年 12 月 22 日　　江苏省政府办公厅出台《关于促进房地产市场健康发展的意见》（苏政办发〔2008〕133 号），提出加大廉租房建设力度、加快推进经济适用房建设，全面实施城市危旧房（棚户区）改造，鼓励支持普通商品房消费，认真落实住房转让相关优惠政策，调整完善拆迁补偿安置政策，支持房地产企业管理融资需求，切实改善对房地产企业服务和进一步加强对房地产市场的监测和管理。

December 22, 2008   Jiangsu Provincial Government Office promulgated "Opinions on Promoting the Real Estate Market to Develop Soundly" (Su Zheng Ban Fa〔2008〕No. 133), proposing to strengthen the construction of low-rental housing, speed up the construction of affordable housing, implement renovation of urban dilapidated buildings (shanty towns) in an all-round manner, encourage and support ordinary commodity housing consumption, seriously implement the preferential policy on housing transfer, adjust and improve the demolition compensation and relocation policy, support real estate enterprises on financing, improve the real estate enterprise services effectively and enhance the monitoring and management of the real estate market.

2009年2月6日   省城市住房与房地产工作领导小组发文明确将省房地产发展与房地产市场调控联席会议调整为省城市住房与房地产工作领导小组，并调整组成单位及人员名单。

February 6, 2009   The Provincial Urban Housing and Real Estate Work Leading Group issued a document to adjust the provincial joint conference on real estate industry development and real estate market regulation to be the Provincial Urban Housing and Real Estate Work Leading Group and adjusted the member units and individuals.

2009年10月14日   国家七部委印发《关于利用住房公积金贷款支持保障性住房建设试点工作的实施意见》（建金〔2009〕160号）。无锡市为江苏省第一家试点城市发放住房公积金贷款3亿元用于经济适用房惠景家园的建设，期限3年，安全收回。

October 14, 2009   The seven ministries and commissions issued "Opinions on Implementation of Pilot Construction of Subsidized Housing by Use of Housing Provident Fund Loans" (Jian Jin〔2009〕No. 160).As Jiangsu's first pilot city, Wuxi granted a total of housing provident fund loans of 300 million *yuan* for construction of the affordable housing project Huijing Jiayuan for a term of three years and the loans had been recovered safely.

2009年12月   省住房城乡建设厅牵头多部门联合出台《关于促进市场平稳健康发展的指导意见》（苏建房〔2009〕395号），要求保持房价稳定。

December 2009   The Provincial Department of Housing and Urban-Rural Development led a few other departments to jointly issue "Guiding Opinions on Promotion of the Steady and Sound Development of Real Estate Market" (Su Jian Fang〔2009〕No. 395), requiring to keep housing prices stable.

2009年12月15日　　江苏省人民政府办公厅印发《江苏省住房和城乡建设厅主要职责内设机构和人员编制规定》（苏政办发〔2009〕141号），主要职责包括承担保障全省城镇低收入家庭住房的责任，推进全省住房制度改革的责任，规范房地产市场秩序、监督管理房地产市场的责任，负责住房公积金监督管理，确保公积金的有效使用和安全。

December 15, 2009　　Jiangsu Provincial People's Government issued "Regulations on Main Responsibilities, Organizational Structure, and Staffing of Jiangsu Provincial Department of Housing and Urban-Rural Development" (Su Zheng Ban Fa〔2009〕No. 141). It is provided that the main duties of such department include guaranteeing the housing of low-income families in urban areas of Jiangsu, promoting the provincial housing system reform, regulating the real estate market order, exercising supervision and management of the real estate market, and supervising the housing provident fund to ensure it to be used in an effective and safe manner.

2010年1月14日　　江苏省人民政府办公厅出台《关于促进房地产市场平稳健康发展的通知》（苏政办发〔2010〕13号），遏制部分城市房价过快上涨的势头。

January 14, 2010　　Jiangsu Provincial People's Government Office issued "Notice on Promoting the Real Estate Market to Develop in a Steady and Healthy Manner" (Su Zheng Ban Fa〔2010〕No. 13) in an effort to keep home prices from rising too quickly in popular cities.

2010年5月　　江苏省住房保障管理信息系统投用使用。

May 2010　　Jiangsu Province Housing Security Management Information System was put into use.

2010年5月7日　　江苏省地方标准《成品住房装修技术标准》（DGJ32/J99–2010）由江苏省住房和城乡建设厅公告发布，自2010年6月1日起施行。

May 7, 2010   Jiangsu Province's local standard "Technical Standard on Decoration of Finished Housing"(DGJ32/J99-2010) was released by Jiangsu Provincial Department of Housing and Urban-Rural Development and it should be implemented since June 1, 2010.

2010 年 6 月 28 日   江苏省住房和城乡建设厅转发《江苏省"优秀住宅示范工程"及"成品住房装修示范工程"管理办法》（苏建函房管〔2010〕501 号）。

June 28, 2010   Jiangsu Provincial Department of Housing and Urban-Rural Development disseminated "Measures of Jiangsu Province on Administration of 'Excellent Housing Demonstration Project' and 'Finished Housing Decoration Demonstration Project'" (Su Jian Han Fang Guan〔2010〕No. 501).

2010 年 8 月   国务院在常州召开保障性安居工程建设工作座谈会，中共中央政治局常委、国务院副总理李克强到会作重要讲话。

August 2010   The State Council held a symposium on the construction of affordable housing projects in Changzhou. At the symposium, Comrade Li Keqiang, serving as a member of the Standing Committee of the Political Bureau of the CPC Central Committee and Vice Premier of the State Council, made an important speech.

2010 年 12 月 1 日   《商品房屋租赁管理办法》经住房和城乡建设部第 12 次部常务会议审议通过，以第 6 号部令发布，自 2011 年 2 月 1 日起施行。

December 1,2010   "The Administrative Measures for the Management of Commercial Housing Leases" was adopted by the 12th Ministry Executive Meeting of the Ministry of Housing and Urban-Rural Development of the People's Republic of China, was promulgated as Decree No. 10 and effective as of February 1, 2011.

2010 年底   全省超额完成住房保障"三年行动计划（2008—2010）"任务，累计新开工各类保障性住房 43.1 万套，发放廉租住房租赁补贴 6.4 万户，完成棚户区危旧房改造 40 万户，解决 89.5 万户城镇家庭的住房困难，实现了城镇低保住房困难家庭申请廉租住房实物配租和租赁补贴、城镇低收入家庭申请购买经济适用住房和廉租住房租赁补贴两个"应保尽保"。

End of 2010　Jiangsu Province over-fulfilled its "Three-Year Action Plan (2008—2010)" on housing security that it had completed cumulative new construction of various types of subsidized housing of 431,000 units, granted low-rental housing rental subsidies to a total of 64,000 homes, completed the renovation of the old and dilapdated housing in shanty towns for 400,000 households, solved the housing difficulties of 895,000 urban households, and achieved the provision of low-rental housing with rents collected or rental subsidies for the urban entitled families receiving subsistence allowances with the housing difficulties and approving urban low-income families to apply for purchase of affordable housing or granting them rental subsidies for low-rental housing.

2011 年起　江苏建立省级保障性住房建设引导资金补助制度，到 2015 年，省级财政累计拨付保障性住房专项引导资金约 36 亿元。建立保障性安居工程新增建设用地计划单列、优先供应机制，到 2015 年，累计安排新增建设用地 6 万亩。

Since 2011　Jiangsu established its provincial subsidized housing construction guiding fund subsidy system. By 2015, the provincial fiscal allotment of the guiding funds dedicated for the construction of subsidized housing amounted to 3.6 billion *yuan*. It also established the mechanism to provide special designation and give priority to supply of incremental land for development of subsidized housing projects and a total of 60,000 *mu* increased construction land had been supplied by 2015.

2011 年 1 月 20 日　《房地产经纪管理办法》经住房和城乡建设部第 65 次部常务会议审议通过，并经国家发展和改革委员会、人力资源和社会保障部同意，自 2011 年 4 月 1 日起施行。

January 20, 2011　"The Administrative Measures for Real Estate Brokerage" was adopted by the 65th Ministry Executive Meeting of the Ministry of Housing and Urban-Rural Development of the People's Republic of China, approved by the National Development and Reform Commission and the Ministry of Human Resources and Social Security, and effective as of April 1, 2011.

2011 年 1 月 21 日　国务院总理温家宝签署国务院第 590 号令，颁布并施行《国有土地上房屋征收与补偿条例》。

January 21, 2011　　Premier Wen Jiabao signed the No. 590 Order of the State Council, promulgating and implementing the "Regulations on the Expropriation and Compensation of Housing on State-Owned Land".

2011年1月31日　　江苏省政府办公厅贯彻国务院办公厅要求，出台《关于进一步做好房地产市场调控工作有关问题的通知》（苏政办发〔2011〕9号），要求巩固和扩大调控成果，省内南京、无锡、苏州、徐州等四个城市陆续实施住房限购政策。

January 31, 2011　　In response to the requirements of the General Office of the State Council, Jiangsu Provincial Government Office issued "Notice on Issues Concerning Further Regulation and Control of the Real Estate Market"(Su Zheng Ban Fa〔2011〕No. 9), requiring consolidation and expansion of the regulation and control results, and Nanjing, Wuxi, Suzhou and Xuzhou had implemented the policy of restricting the purchase of housing properties.

2011年2月1日　　省政府办公厅印发《关于认真贯彻实施〈自有土地上房屋征收与补偿条例〉切实做好房屋征收与补偿工作的通知》（苏政传发〔2011〕24号）。

February 1, 2011　　The Office of Jiangsu Provincial Government issued the "Notice on the Earnest Implementation of 'House Acquisition from Private Land and Compensation Ordinance' and the Implementation of the Work of House Acquisition and Compensation" (Su Zheng Chuan Fa〔2011〕No. 24)..

2011年2月18日　　江苏省人民政府办公厅转发省住房和城乡建设厅等部门《关于加快推进成品住房开发建设的实施意见》（苏政办发〔2011〕14号）。

February 18, 2011　　Jiangsu Provincial People's Government Office disseminated "Implementation Opinions on Accelerating the Development and Construction of Finished Housing" (Su Zheng Ban Fa〔2011〕No. 14) that was prepared by Jiangsu Provincial Department of Housing and Urban-Rural Development and other authorities.

2011年6月25日　　江苏省政府第73号令《江苏省公共租赁住房管理办法》发布，首次以政府令形式明确把城市中等偏下收入住房困难家庭、新就业和外来务工人员纳入公共租赁住房保障范围。

June 25, 2011   Jiangsu Provincial Government promulgated its Decree No. 73 "Measures of Jiangsu Province on Administration of Public Rental Housing" and it was the first time that it was clearly provided in the form of the government decree to bring the lower moderate-income urban families with housing difficulties, new entrants to the labor force and migrant workers into the public rental housing coverage.

2011 年 7 月 1 日起   全省机关事业单位住房公积金单位和个人缴存比例分别调整为 12%。

Since July 1, 2011   The depositing percentages of the housing provident fund by the units and the individuals of the government departments and institutions in Jiangsu were adjusted to be 12% respectively.

2011 年 7 月 8 日   省政府印发《江苏省贯彻实施〈国有土地上房屋征收与补偿条例〉若干问题规定的通知》（苏政发〔2011〕91 号）。

July 8, 2011   The Provincial Government issued the "Notice on Several Regulations on Issues of the Implementation of 'House Acquisition from State-Owned Land and Compensation Ordinance'" (Su Zheng Fa〔2011〕No. 91).

2011 年 7 月   全国人大调研组来江苏调研保障性住房建设情况，听取省政府和省住建厅、发改委、财政厅、国土厅有关工作情况汇报。

July 2011   The National People's Congress Research Group came to Jiangsu to investigate the construction of affordable housing and listen to the reports of Jiangsu Provincial Government, Jiangsu Provincial Department of Housing and Urban-Rural Development, the Provincial Development and Reform Commission, the Provincial Department of Finance and the Provincial Department of Land and Resources.

2011 年 8 月 19 日   中共江苏省委、江苏省人民政府出台《关于大力推进民生幸福工程的意见》，把"完善住房保障体系"列入全省民生幸福工程六大体系之一，要求坚持增加投入与创新机制并重，大力发展公共租赁住房，形成多渠道、多形式解决群众住房困难的住房保障体系。

August 19, 2011   The CPC Provincial Committee and the Provincial People's Government of Jiangsu issued "Opinions on Vigorous Promotion of People's Wellbeing Program" to list "improving the housing security system" as one of the six systems of the provincial people's wellbeing program, requiring paying equal attention to increasing the income and innovating the mechanism, vigorously developing the public rental housing and forming a housing security system with a wide range of channels and forms to solve the people's housing difficulties.

2011 年 9 月 7 日   江苏在全国率先对住房保障体系进行"系统化设计、制度化安排、规范化建设和长效化推进"。省政府《关于进一步加强住房保障体系建设的实施意见》（苏政发〔2011〕126 号）确定了我省住房保障体系的基本框架、主要内容和重点任务。

September 7, 2011   Jiangsu got ahead in carrying out "systematic design, institutional arrangements, regulated construction and long-term promotion" of the housing security system. Jiangsu Provincial People's Government issued "Opinions on Further Strengthening of Housing Security System Construction" (Su Zheng Fa〔2011〕No. 126) to clearly provide the basic framework, main contents and key tasks of the housing security system of Jiangsu.

2011 年 11 月 25 日   江苏省人民代表大会常务委员会开展首次专题询问工作，住房保障被列为第一项专题询问事项。

November 25, 2011   Jiangsu Provincial People's Congress Standing Committee carried out the first special inquiry activity and housing security was listed as the province's first special inquiry.

2011 年 12 月 8 日   中共江苏省委办公厅、江苏省人民政府办公厅印发《全省美好城乡建设行动实施方案》（苏办发〔2011〕55 号），明确将各市成品住房发展比例指标，纳入省委省政府对各市市委市政府的考核范围。

December 8, 2011   CPC Jiangsu Provincial Committee Office and Jiangsu Provincial People's Government Office issued "Executive Plan for Provincial Program on Construction of Beautiful Urban and Rural Areas" (Su Ban Fa〔2011〕No. 55) to provide clearly that the finished housing development proportion of each city would be brought into the assessment scope of the CPC municipal committee and the municipal government by CPC Jiangsu Provincial Committee and Jiangsu Provincial Government.

2011年　建立了省级保障性住房建设引导资金补助制度，省级财政累计拨付保障性住房专项引导资金约 36 亿元。

2011　A provincial guiding fund subsidy system for construction of subsidized housing was established. The provincial fiscal had allotted a total of about 3.6 billion *yuan* as the special guiding fund for construction of subsidized housing.

2012年5月　常州市在江苏全省率先开展公共租赁住房筹集方式创新试点，按照保障家庭需求从市场租赁存量商品住房用作公共租赁住房，（2012年6月初至2016上半年）累计共筹集 3300 套（该数字已与常州房管局保障处核实），该模式后被住建部向全国推广（《长期租赁社会房源实施公租房保障取得多快好省成效》纳入 2014 年 11 月住建部《全国住房保障工作经验交流专辑》在全国推广）。

May 2012　Changzhou took the lead in piloting the innovation on raising public rental housing that it leased commodity housing in stock from the market as public rental housing resources to meet the demands of the subsidized families and it had raised a total of 3,300 units for the period from early June 2012 to the first half of 2016 (this figure had been verified with the Security Office of Changzhou Housing Administration). This pattern was later popularized nationwide by the Ministry of Housing and Urban-Rural Development (and the paper "Long-term Leasing of Social Housing Sources for Provision of Public Rental Housing Security Performing Effectively" was included in *National Housing Security Experience Exchange Album* for nationwide promotion).

2012年6月15日　江苏省住房和城乡建设厅转发住房和城乡建设部《关于推进国有土地上房屋征收与补偿信息公开工作的实施意见》（苏建房管〔2012〕349 号），对房屋征收信息公开制度建设、公开渠道与内容、公开工作考评和监督明确了规定和要求。

June 15, 2012　Jiangsu Provincial Department of Housing and Urban-Rural Development disseminated "Implementation Opinions on Pushing Forward Information Disclosure of Requisition and Compensation of Housing Built on State-Owned Land" (Su Jian Fang Guan〔2012〕No. 349) to give clear provisions and requirements on construction of the housing requisition information disclosure system, channels and contents of disclosure, assessment and supervision of disclosure.

2012年7月7日　　中共中央政治局常委、国务院总理温家宝赴常州调研住房保障工作。温家宝主持召开座谈会，听取江苏省住房和城乡建设厅厅长周岚和徐州、常州、扬州市住房保障主管部门负责人有关工作情况的汇报，并与保障对象代表亲切交谈。

July 7, 2012　　Wen Jiabao, the member of the CPC Central Committee Political Bureau Standing Committee & Premier of the State Council went to Changzhou to study the housing security work. Wen Jiabao presided over a symposium, listening to the work reports of Director Zhou Lan of Jiangsu Provincial Department of Housing and Urban-Rural Development and the leaders of the competent housing security authorities of Xuzhou, Changzhou and Yangzhou and talking with the representatives of the subsidized groups warmly.

2012年8月　　江苏在全国率先开展住房保障体系建设试点示范创建工作，着力通过破解难点难题促进住房保障体系完善。

August 2012　　Jiangsu took the lead domestically in carrying out the housing security system construction pilot and demonstration work with efforts made on removing difficulties to promote the improvement of the housing security system.

2013年6月13日　　江苏在全国率先设立"住房保障体系健全率"综合指标，2013年6月13日纳入对市县民生幸福工程考核评价体系和"两个率先"进程监测统计体系。"两个率先"进程监测统计体系为：江苏省全面建成小康社会指标体系、江苏基本实现现代化指标体系。

June 13, 2013　　Jiangsu took the lead domestically in establishing the composite indicator of "housing security system soundness rate" and bringing it into the municipal/county people's wellbeing program assessment system and the "two leads" process monitoring and statistics system on June 13, 2013.The "two leads" process monitoring and statistics system means: The indicator system for Jiangsu to build itself a moderately prosperous society and the indicator system for Jiangsu to achieve modernization basically.

2013年8月21日　　江苏省人民政府出台《关于加快棚户区（危旧房）改造工作的实施意见》（苏政发〔2013〕108号），对棚户区改造的总体要求、目标任务、基本原则、支持政策首次做出全面部署。

August 21, 2013   Jiangsu Provincial People's Government issued "Opinions on Acceleration of Renovation of Shanty Towns (Old and Dilapidated Buildings)" (Su Zheng Fa〔2013〕No.108) to cover the general requirements, objectives and tasks, basic principles, and support policies for renovation of shanty towns in an all-around manner for the first time.

2013年12月6日   中央机构编制委员会办公室下发《中央编办关于整合不动产登记职责的通知》（中央编办发〔2013〕134号），将房屋登记职责整合到国土不动产登记部门。

December 6, 2013   The State Commission Office for Public Sector Reform issued "Notice of the State Commission Office of Public Sector Reform on the Integration of the Responsibility for the Registration of Immovable Property" (Issued by State Commission Office for Public Sector Reform〔2013〕No.134), integrating the responsibilities for the housing registration into the Real Estate Registration Department.

2014年1月13日   江苏省住房和城乡建设厅、江苏省财政厅、江苏省发展改革委联合印发《关于全面推进公共租赁住房和廉租住房并轨运行的实施意见》，到2015年年底，全省所有市县实现"两房"并轨运行。

January 13, 2014   Jiangsu Provincial Department of Housing and Urban-Rural Development, Jiangsu Provincial Department of Finance, and Jiangsu Provincial Development and Reform Commission jointly issued "Implementation Opinions on Promotion of Integrated Operation of Public Rental Housing and Low-rental Housing in an All-round Manner" and as of the end of 2015, all cities and counties in Jiangsu had achieved the said integrated operation.

2014年3月   江苏省建立省市房地产市场监测分析联动工作机制。自7月起，实施限购的南京、无锡、苏州、徐州等四个城市陆续调整限购政策，当年全面取消限购。

March 2014   Jiangsu Province established the provincial and municipal real estate market monitoring and analysis linkage mechanism. Nanjing, Wuxi, Suzhou and Xuzhou that implemented the restriction on housing purchase had adjusted their restriction on housing purchase policies in succession since July and revoked such polices in an all-around manner in the same year.

2014年4月23日   江苏省编委下发《关于整合不动产登记职责的通知》（苏编〔2014〕11号）。

April 23, 2014　　Jiangsu Province Committee Office for Public Sector Reform issued "Notice on the Integration of Responsibilities for Real Estate Registration" (Su Bian〔2014〕No.11).

2014年5月7日　　江苏省住房和城乡建设厅、江苏省财政厅印发《江苏省住宅专项维修资金管理办法》（苏建房管〔2014〕208号）。

May 7, 2014　　Jiangsu Provincial Department of Housing and Urban-Rural Development and Jiangsu Provincial Department of Finance issued "Measures of Jiangsu Province on Administration of Special Housing Maintenance Fund" (Su Jian Fang Guan〔2014〕No. 208).

2014年10月31日　　《省政府关于加快推进建筑产业现代化促进建筑产业转型升级的意见》（苏政发〔2014〕111号）下发实施，明确以发展绿色建筑为方向，以住宅产业现代化为重点，以新型建筑工业化为手段，"三位一体"统筹推进全省建筑产业现代化。

October 31, 2014　　"Opinions of Jiangsu Provincial Government on Accelerating Promotion of Modernization of the Construction Industry for Its Transformation and Upgrading" (Su Zheng Fa〔2014〕No. 111) was issued to specify the unified promotion of the modernization of the construction industry across the whole province by taking green buildings as the direction, focusing on modernization of the residential industry and by means of new type industrialization of construction.

2014年11月24日　　国务院总理李克强签署中华人民共和国国务院令第656号，公布《不动产登记条例》，自2015年3月1日起施行。

November 24, 2014　　Premier of the State Council Li Keqiang signed Decree No. 656 of the State Council, promulgating the "Real Estate Registration Ordinance" which was effective as of March 1, 2015.

2014年12月2日　　省住房城乡建设厅、省财政厅、省国土资源厅、省物价局联合印发《关于推进保障性住房共有产权工作的意见》（苏建房保〔2014〕671号）。淮安市成为全国共有产权住房六个试点城市之一。"目标明确、制度健全，政策落实、机制完善，进退有序、管理规范"的具有江苏特点的住房保障体系初步建成。

December 2, 2014   The Provincial Department of Housing and Urban-Rural Development, the Provincial Department of Finance, the Provincial Department of Land and Resources and the Provincial Price Bureau jointly issued "Opinions on Promotion of Development of Joint Property of Subsidized Housing" (Su Jian Fang Bao〔2014〕No. 671). Huai'an became one of the country's designated six cities in piloting joint property of subsidized housing. Jiangsu initially developed its characteristic housing security system featuring "clear targets, sound system, implementation of policies, good mechanism, controlled advance or retreat, and regulated management".

2015 年 1 月 20 日   住房和城乡建设部、财政部、人民银行联合发文《关于放宽提取住房公积金支付房租条件通知》（建金〔2015〕19 号）。规定职工连续足额缴存住房公积金满 3 个月，本人及配偶在缴存城市无自有住房且租赁住房的，可提取夫妻双方公积金支付房租。

January 20, 2015   The Ministry of Housing and Urban-Rural Development, the Ministry of Finance and the People's Bank jointly issued "Notice on Relaxing Restrictions on Withdrawal of Housing Provident Fund to Pay Rental" (Jian Jin〔2015〕No. 19). It is provided that an employee who has paid the housing provident fund for three months or more in succession and the employee and his/her spouse has no own house property but leased an apartment in the housing provident fund paying city, the said couple can draw their housing provident funds to pay the rent.

2015 年 11 月 23 日   江苏省人民政府办公厅印发《关于加快推进棚户区（危旧房）改造货币化安置的意见》（苏政办发〔2015〕119 号）。明确要求自 2016 年起，各市、县（市、区）棚户区（危旧房）改造货币化安置比例原则上不低于 50%。

November 23, 2015   Jiangsu Provincial People's Government Office issued "Guidance Opinions on Vigorous Promotion of Monetized Resettlement for Renovation of Shanty Towns(Old and Dilapidated Buildings)" (Su Zheng Ban Fa〔2015〕No. 119). It clearly required that the monetized resettlement for renovation of shanty towns(old and dilapidated buildings) each city, county (district) should in principle account for a percentage not less than 50%.

2015 年 12 月 15 日   江苏省人民政府办公厅印发《江苏省政府购买棚改服务管理办法 (暂行)》（苏政办发〔2015〕130 号），确定将棚户区改造相关服务事项按照一定的方式和程序，交由具备条件的社会力量和事业单位承担，并由政府根据合同约定向其支付费用。

December 15, 2015　Jiangsu Provincial Government Office issued "Notice on Measures of Jiangsu Provincial Government on Purchase of Shanty Towns Renovation Services (Temporary)" (Su Zheng Ban Fa〔2015〕No. 130), deciding to entrust eligible social forces and public undertakings to render services relating to the renovation of the shanty towns according to a certain mode and procedure, and to pay the costs according to the contracts by the government.

2015 年 12 月 31 日　全省各市县全部建立公共租赁住房制度，90% 的市县实现了城镇住房保障准入标准的动态调整。全省各级受理服务窗口超过 2000 个，比 2010 年增加 4 倍；90% 的市、县实现了收入资产多部门审核，比 2010 年增加 2 倍。2015 年年底，全省住房保障体系健全率超过 88%。

December 31, 2015　All cities and counties in Jiangsu Province had established the public rental housing system, and 90% of them had realized the dynamic adjustment of the urban housing security access standard. Jiangsu Province had more than 2,000 relevant service windows at all levels, an increase of four times over 2010;90% of the cites and counties achieved the multi-sector audit of income assets, an increase of 2 times over 2010. By the end of 2015, the soundness rate of the provincial housing security system exceeded 88%.

2016 年 3 月 7 日　全面实施不动产统一登记制度后，江苏省住房城乡建设厅印发《江苏省住房城乡建设厅关于切实做好房屋交易和产权管理工作的指导意见》（苏建房管〔2016〕80 号），指导各地做好新形势下房屋交易与产权管理工作。

March 7, 2016　After the full implementation of the unified registration system for real estate, Jiangsu Provincial Development of Housing and Urban-Rural Development issued "Instruction of Jiangsu Provincial Development of Housing and Urban-Rural Development on the Implementation of Housing Transactions and Property Management" (Su Jian Fang Guan〔2016〕No. 80), guiding all localities to do a good job in housing transactions and property management in the new situation.

2016 年 3 月 11 日　《江苏省房地产经纪服务标准》通过江苏省工程建设标准验收并发布，自 2016 年 5 月 1 日起实施。该《标准》是江苏省率先在国内房地产经纪行业出台的第一部指导性服务标准。

March 11, 2016　"The Real Estate Brokerage Service Standard in Jiangsu Province" passed the acceptance for engineering construction standards in Jiangsu Province and was issued, being effective as of May 1, 2016. The "Standard" was the first directive service standard launched by Jiangsu Province taking in the domestic real estate brokerage industry.

2016 年 4 月 10 日　　江苏省住房和城乡建设厅发布《江苏省"十三五"物业管理行业发展规划》，明确了"十三五"时期物业管理行业发展的指导思想、总体目标、主要任务和保障措施，是今后五年全省物业管理行业发展的纲领性文件。

April 10, 2016　　Jiangsu Provincial Development of Housing and Urban-Rural Development issued "Development Planning of Jiangsu Province for the Property Management Industry during the '13th Five-Year' Period", defining that the guiding ideology, the overall goal, the main task and safeguard measures of the development of the property management industry during the "13th Five-Year", being the programmatic document for the development of the provincial property management industry during the next five years.

2016 年 4 月　　镇江市住房公积金管理中心下发了《关于镇江市自由职业者个人缴存和使用住房公积金的通知》（镇公积金〔2016〕32 号）。由此，全省多个城市住房公积金管理部门探索建立自由职业者住房公积金缴存机制。

April 2016　　Zhenjiang Housing Provident Fund Management Center issued "Notice on Freelancers's Personal Deposit and Use of Housing Provident Fund in Zhenjiang" (Zhen Housing Provident Fund〔2016〕No. 32). From then on, several urban housing provident fund management departments start to explore the establishment of housing provident fund deposit mechanism by freelancers.

2016 年 5 月 19 日　　江苏省住房和城乡建设厅发布《江苏省"十三五"物业管理行业发展规划》，明确了"十三五"时期江苏省住房和城乡建设厅联合省发展改革委、省财政厅、人民银行南京分行下发《江苏省关于贯彻落实〈关于规范和阶段性适当降低住房公积金缴存比例的通知〉的实施指导意见》（苏建金管〔2016〕218 号）。

May 19, 2016　　Jiangsu Provincial Development of Housing and Urban-Rural Development issued "Development Planning of Jiangsu Province for the Property Management Industry during the '13th Five-Year' Period", defining that Jiangsu Provincial Development of Housing and Urban-Rural Development should work together with the Provincial Development and Reform Commission, the Provincial Department of Finance and the People's Bank of China Nanjing Branch to issue "Guidance of Jiangsu Province on the Implementation of

'Notice on the Standardization and Proper Periodical Reduction of the Deposit Ratio of Housing Provident Fund'" (Su Jian Jin Guan〔2016〕No. 218).

2016年6月7日　江苏省住房和城乡建设厅印发《江苏省住房城乡建设厅关于建设省城镇个人住房信息系统的通知》，全面部署城镇个人住房信息系统建设工作，确定了系统建设的总体目标、工作要求和数据标准，明确了省、市、县三级职责。

June 7, 2016　Jiangsu Provincial Department of Housing and Urban-Rural Development issued "Notice of Jiangsu Provincial Department of Housing and Urban-Rural Development on Building Provincial Urban Individual Housing Information System" in order to fully deploy the construction of the urban individual housing information system, which determined the overall objectives, working requirements and data standards of system construction, and clarified the responsibilities of the province, the city and the county.

2016年6月28日　省住房和城乡建设厅、省财政厅印发《关于下达2016年省级节能减排（建筑产业现代化）专项引导资金的通知》（苏财建〔2016〕120号）。2016年创建省级建筑产业现代化示范城市4个，集成应用类示范基地2个、设计研发类示范基地18个、部品生产类示范基地19个、示范项目8个。

June 28, 2016　Jiangsu Provincial Department of Housing and Urban-Rural Development and Department of Finance of Jiangsu Province issued "Notice on the Special Guiding Fund of Provincial-level Energy Saving and Emission Reduction (Modernization of the Construction Industry)" (Su Cai Jian〔2016〕No.120). In 2016, there were four demonstration cities for the modernization of the provincial-level construction industry, two demonstration bases for integrated application, 18 demonstration bases for design and development, 19 demonstration bases for the production of parts, and eight demonstration projects.

2016年6月30日　盐城市住房公积金管理中心联合阜宁县人民政府印发《阜宁县"新市民"住房公积金缴存使用实施细则》，探索建立进城务工农民建缴住房公积金制度实行财政定额定期补贴试点。住建部相关领导到阜宁开展专题调研，总结江苏做法。

June 30, 2016　Yancheng City Housing Provident Fund Management Center and Funing County People's Government issued "Detailed Rules for the Implementation of the Payment and Use of Housing Provident Fund of 'New Citizen' of Funing County" in order to explore the implementation of housing provident fund system for the rural migrant workers to carry out the

pilots of the fiscal fixed-term subsidy. The relevant leaders of the Ministry of Housing and Urban-Rural Development went to Funing to carry out special research and summarize the practice of Jiangsu.

2016 年 6—11 月　　根据住房城乡建设部的部署并结合江苏省实际，在全省开展了房地产开发经营行为专项检查和房地产中介行业专项整治工作，严厉打击房地产开发企业不正当经营行为和房地产中介机构违法违规行为。

During June to November of 2016　　According to the deployment of the Ministry of Housing and Urban-Rural Development and combining the actual situation of Jiangsu Province, the special inspection for real estate development and operation behavior and the specific rectification for the real estate intermediate industry were developed in Jiangsu Province to crack down on illegal competition of the real estate development enterprises and the illegal behavior of the real estate intermediaries.

2016 年 7 月 29 日　　住房和城乡建设部等 9 部门下发了《关于加强房地产中介管理促进行业健康发展的意见》，进一步规范中介服务行为，加强行业管理，保护群众合法权益，促进行业健康发展。

July 29, 2016　　The Ministry of Housing and Urban-Rural Development and other eight departments issued "Opinions on Strengthening the Management of Real Estate Intermediary and Promoting the Health Development of the Industry" to further standardize the intermediary service behavior, strengthen the management of the industry, protect the legal interest of the people, and promote the healthy development of the industry.

2016 年 8 月 17 日　　江苏省住房和城乡建设厅印发《江苏省装配式建筑（混凝土结构）施工图审查导则（试行）》（苏建函科〔2016〕565 号），填补了国内空白。

Aug. 17, 2016　　Jiangsu Provincial Department of Housing and Urban-Rural Development issued "Guidelines for the Review of Construction Drawing of Fabricated Structure (Concrete Structure) in Jiangsu Province (Trial Implementation)" (Su Jian Han Ke〔2016〕No.565), which filled the domestic void.

2016 年 10 月 11 日　　江苏省住房公积金系统被江苏省文明委命名为"江苏省文明行业"。开创江苏住建系统机关内设处室首个文明行业先河。

Oct. 11, 2016　　Jiangsu Province Housing Provident Fund System was named "Jiangsu Civilized Industry" by Jiangsu Civilization Committee. This behavior pioneered the first civilized industry in the offices and departments of Jiangsu housing system.

2016年11月3日　　江苏省住房和城乡建设厅发布《江苏省房地产估价报告评审标准（试行）》，进一步加强对全省房地产估价机构和注册房地产估价师执业行为的管理，提高全省房地产估价报告质量，规范全省房地产估价行业的发展。

October 31, 2014　　Jiangsu Provincial Department of Housing and Urban-Rural Development issued "Standard of Report Evaluation for Real Estate Appraisal of Jiangsu Province (Trial Implementation)". It further strengthened the management of the real estate appraisal institutions and the conduct of certified real estate appraiser in the whole province, improved the quality of the real estate appraisal report of the whole province, and standardized the development of the real estate appraisal industry in the whole province.

2016年11月3—5日　　第九届江苏省国际绿色建筑大会在南京国际博览中心成功举办。大会设立建筑产业现代化、海绵城市与城市水环境等多个专题论坛，重点探讨生态城市、绿色建筑和装配式建筑主题。

November 3-5, 2016　　The Ninth Jiangsu International Conference on Green Building was successfully held in Nanjing International Expo Center. The conference established a number of thematic forums such as building industry modernization, sponge city and urban water environment, focusing on the theme of eco-city, green building and fabricated building.

2016年11月10日　　全国首个采用预制集成模块建筑建设的示范项目 —— 镇江新区港南路公租房六号楼通过主体验收。镇江港南路公租房项目为10幢18层建筑，建筑面积13.4万平方米。

Nov. 10, 2016　　The first demonstration project adopting the construction of prefabricated integrated module building in the country — the No.6 Building of Public Rental Housing at Gangnan Road, Zhenjiang Economic and Technological Development Zone was checked and accepted by the main body. The project of public rental housing of Gangnan Road of Zhenjiang had 10 buildings with 18 stories each, with the building area of 134,000 m^2.

2016年11月16日　江苏省住房和城乡建设厅召开全省适老住区建设试点示范推进会暨现场经验交流会。落实《省政府办公厅关于开展适宜养老住区建设试点示范工作的通知》(苏政办发〔2015〕120号)文件要求，研究部署全省推进适老住区建设工作，并对工作中的重点和难点问题进行交流探讨。

Nov. 16, 2016　Jiangsu Provincial Department of Housing and Urban-Rural Development held the Meeting of Promoting the Pilot Demonstration of the Construction of the Suitable Residential House for the Elderly in the Province and On-site Experience Exchange Meeting. The meeting implemented the requirements of the "Notice of Jiangsu Provincial Government on Carrying out the Pilot Demonstration of Suitable Residential House for the Elderly" (Su Zheng Ban Fa〔2015〕No.120), researched and deployed the whole province to promote the construction of the suitable residential area for the elderly, and conducted communication and discussion on the key and difficult problems in the work.

2016年12月1日　《中华人民共和国资产评估法》正式施行。

Dec. 1, 2016　"The Asset Appraisal Law of the People's Republic of China" was formally implemented.

2016年12月　江苏省统计局通过计算机辅助电话调查系统（CATI），在各设区市采用配额抽样和简单随机抽样方法抽取12558人，就全省"民生幸福工程六大体系"（终身教育、就业服务、社会保障、基本医疗卫生、住房保障、社会养老服务）进行满意度调查，已公布的结果显示各地群众对住房的满意度达到86.6%，满意度领先于其他五大体系。

December 2016　Based on the Computer Assisted Telephone Interviewing System (CATI), the Jiangsu Provincial Bureau of Statistics selected 12,558 persons by using quota sampling and simple random sampling method to investigate the satisfaction for the six systems of livelihood happiness project (lifelong education, employment services, social security, basic medical care and health, housing security and social pension services) of the province. The results showed that the satisfaction of the masses to the housing reached 86.6%, which was ahead of the other five systems.

2017年2月23日　江苏省住房和城乡建设厅联合省高级人民法院出台了《关于建立住房公积金

执行联动机制的指导意见》，进一步规范涉及住房公积金案件执行程序。

Feb. 23, 2017 Jiangsu Provincial Department of Housing and Urban-Rural Development and Jiangsu Higher People's Court jointly issued "Guidance on the Establishment of Executive Linkage Mechanism of Housing Provident Fund" to further regulate the implementation procedure involving the housing provident fund cases.

2017 年 2 月 根据住建部要求，江苏省住房和城乡建设厅及时下发《关于适时调整住房公积金政策确保房地产市场平稳健康发展的通知》（苏建传〔2017〕4 号），发挥了住房公积金对稳定市场，支持住房合理消费的作用。

February 2017 According to the requirements of the Ministry of Housing and Urban-Rural Development, Jiangsu Provincial Department of Housing and Urban-Rural Development timely issued "Notice on Timely Adjustment of Housing Provident Fund Policy to Ensure the Stable and Healthy Development of the Real Estate Market" (Su Jian Chuan〔2017〕No.4), having played the role of housing provident fund in stabilizing the market and the function of supporting the reasonable consumption of housing.

2017 年 5 月 2 日 江苏省住房城乡建设厅印发《关于进一步加强城镇退役军人住房保障工作的通知》（苏建房保〔2017〕197 号），要求各地进一步完善住房保障政策体系，确保城镇专业士官、退役士兵和伤病残军人纳入各地住房保障体系，对其中符合当地住房保障条件的要给予优先保障。

May 2, 2017 Jiangsu Provincial Department of Housing and Urban-Rural Development issued "Notice on Further Strengthening the Housing Guarantee of Urban Ex-serviceman"(Su Jian Fang Bao〔2017〕No.197), requesting all local authorities to further improve the housing security policy system so as to ensure the urban professional officers, retired soldiers and disabled soldiers were incorporate into the housing security system, and give priority to the person who conformed to the local housing guarantee conditions.

2017 年 5 月 18 日 江苏省住房和城乡建设厅发布《关于开展培育和发展住房租赁市场试点工作的通知》，确定了搭建住房租赁信息政府服务平台、培育专业化住房租赁机构、推进住房租赁规模化经营三种试点模式，选定南京市、苏州市、无锡市、常州市、徐州市、扬州市率先开展培育和发展住房租赁市场工作。

May 18, 2017　Jiangsu Provincial Department of Housing and Urban-Rural Development issued "Notice on Developing the Pilot Work of the Cultivation and Development of Housing Leasing Market", which established three pilot patterns including the establishment of government service platform of housing leasing information, the cultivation of specialized housing leasing institutions, and the advancement of the large-scale operation of housing leasing. And Nanjing, Suzhou, Wuxi, Changzhou, Xuzhou, Yangzhou were selected to carry out the cultivation and development of the housing rental market at first.

2017 年 5 月 24 日　江苏省住房城乡建设厅印发《关于进一步加强农民工住房工作的意见》（苏建房保〔2017〕242 号）。要求各地按照稳步推进城镇基本公共服务常住人口全覆盖的总体要求，加快将农民工纳入城镇住房保障体系，把在城镇具有稳定职业的农民工纳入住房保障范围，切实降低门槛，将农民工住房保障工作纳入制度化、规范化轨道。

May 24, 2017　Jiangsu Provincial Department of Housing and Urban-Rural Development issued "Opinions on Further Strengthening the Housing Work of Rural Migrant Workers"(Su Jian Fang Bao〔2017〕No.242), requesting all localities, in accordance with the overall requirements of steadily advancing the full coverage of urban basic public service permanent residents, to incorporate the rural migrant workers into the urban housing security system, to accelerate the integration of rural migrant workers into the urban housing security system, to incorporate the rural migrant workers with steady job into the scope of housing security, to effectively reduce the threshold, and to integrate the housing security work of rural migrant workers into institutionalized and standardized tracks.

2017 年 6 月　江苏省各地全面接入全国住房公积金异地转移接续平台，为住房公积金缴存职工办理异地转移接续业务提供了便利。

June 2017　All localities of Jiangsu Province fully accessed the off-site transfer connection platform of national housing provident fund, which provided convenience for the staff to deposite the housing provident fund and handle the off-site transfer connection business.

2017年8月1日　　江苏省住房和城乡建设厅发布《江苏省住宅产业现代化"十三五"发展规划》，明确了"十三五"期间江苏省住宅产业现代化的发展目标、任务、具体举措和实施保障。

Aug. 1, 2017　　Jiangsu Provincial Department of Housing and Urban-Rural Development issued "Development Planning of Jiangsu Province for the modernization of Housing Industry during the '13th Five-Year' Period", and defined the development goals, tasks, specific measures and implementation guarantee for the modernization of housing industry in Jiangsu Province during the period of "13th Five-year" plan.

2017年8月25日　　《江苏省人民政府办公厅关于提升社区物业服务水平 促进现代物业服务业发展的指导意见》出台，对破解江苏省物业服务业发展瓶颈问题，引导企业转型升级，加强对业主自治的管理监督等提出了明确要求。

Aug. 25, 2017　　"Guiding Opinions of Jiangsu Provincial People's Government on Improving Community Property Service Level and Promoting the Development of Modern Property Service Industry" was issued, which made clear requirements on solving the bottleneck problem of the development of property service industry in Jiangsu, guiding the transformation and upgrading of enterprises, and strengthening the management and supervision of proprietors' self-government.

后记

　　为了系统记录和反映改革开放以来江苏住房发展变迁历程及取得的巨大成就，引导全社会正确认识理解解决住有所居世界性难题的艰巨性复杂性，2015 年 12 月，江苏省住房和城乡建设厅启动了《江苏住房变迁纪实（1978—2017）》图册视频短片编制工作。一年多来，编委会共召集成员处室单位主要负责人及联络员召开了 12 次专题会议，就该图册短片编制的工作思路、定位、框架方案、篇章结构、重点内容、表现手法、实施方法步骤等重大问题，组织深入讨论、渐次推进、逐步深化，确保了整个编制工作有序顺利开展。厅住宅与房地产业促进中心作为该图册短片编制承担执行单位，抽调专门精干力量组成编制工作推进小组，在"不动用或少动用行政力量"、无经验可循、无资料积累的情况下，克服困难，想方设法，与鼎艺国际、常州城建影视 2 个专业公司紧密协作，较为圆满地完成了江苏第一部经过系统梳理、较为全面反映改革开放 40 年来江苏住房发展变迁历程及巨大成就的图册短片编制任务，基本实现了江苏省住房和城乡建设厅当初确定的预期目标。

　　由于本图册短片反映江苏住房发展的方方面面，内容多、时间跨度大，图片资料采集甄选难免有疏漏，加之成稿仓促，受编制水平的局限，如有编者未联系到的图片资料作者，请与编者及时取得联系，以便编者致谢；有失偏颇、不妥之处，敬请专家、读者批评指正。

　　感谢中国房地产业协会副会长、秘书长冯俊，原江苏省建设委员会巡视员徐益民，江苏省住房和城乡建设厅原副巡视员赵华中，中国房地产业协会副会长、原南京市房产管理局副局长胡志刚，南京市房地产业协会秘书长曾新骏，各市县住建主管部门和有关企业，陆志刚工作团队、杜俊工作团队，在开展专访、图片资料提供、场景拍摄等工作开展方面给予的大力支持和帮助。

编　者

2017 年 11 月

Postscript

In December 2015, Jiangsu Provincial Department of Housing and Urban-Rural Development launched the preparation work of atlas and short video of *Documentary on the Evolution of Residential Housing in Jiangsu (1978—2017)* in order to systematically record and reflect the great achievements of the changes course of housing development in Jiangsu since the reform and opening up, and guide the whole society to understand the difficulty and complexity of solving the world's problem that "everyone has a house". For more than a year, the Editorial Board has assembled main responsible persons and liaison officers of the member's office units to convene 12 special meetings, organizing to deep discuss, gradually boost and gradually deepen the major issues of the atlas and short video including work ideas, positioning, framework programs, text structure, key content, expression techniques and implementation methods so as to ensured that the whole preparation work was carried out smoothly. The execution units of the short film are Housing and Real Estate Promotion Center, Jiangsu Provincial Department of Housing and Urban-Rural Development. To produce the short film, the center selected the keen-witted and capable force to form the compilation working group members. Under the circumstance of having no experience to follow and no accumulated material to use, the center tried not to use our administrative power, looked for every ways, overcame many difficulties, and closely cooperated with two professional companies "Do Enjoy Company" and "Changzhou Chengjian Studio". Finally, the center completed the mission of making the short film and achieved the expected goal that was set by Jiangsu Provincial Department of Housing and Urban-Rural Development. This is the first short film that comprehensively and systematically reflects the change and great achievements of the Department over the past 40 years since reform and opening-up.

The short film reflects every aspect of Jiangsu's housing development, which has a large number of contents and a long time span. At the same time, due to the limitation of the auditing level and the limited time, the selection of the photos may have some careless omissions, the authors of some photos may be not noted clearly. If you find some problems, please contact with the editors to make the proper acknowledgement. The team is open to all advices and suggestions.

Thanks to Feng Jun, vice president, secretary general of China Real Estate Association, Xu Yimin, former inspector of Construction Commission of Jiangsu Province, Zhao Huazhong, former vice inspector of Jiangsu Provincial Department of Housing and Urban-Rural Development, Hu Zhigang, vice president of Nanjing Real Estate Association, former deputy director of Administrative Bureau of House Property, Zeng Xinjun, secretary general of Nanjing Real Estate Association, competent departments of cities and counties, companies concerned, Huzhigang Team, Dujun Team, for all of your substantial support and help in the aspects of conducting exclusive interview, the offer of relevant photos and materials, shooting and so on.

The Editor

November 2017

《江苏住房变迁纪实 (1978-2017)》(DVD) 内容简介

　　改革开放四十周年，江苏住房发展成就文献资料——《广厦欢颜——江苏住房变迁纪实（1978-2017）》短片，以时间脉络为线索，通过老百姓讲身边住房故事、住房专家和领导访谈、住区实景拍摄，以及剪辑住房历史影像资料等手法，系统回顾与展现了改革开放四十年来江苏住房，从"三代同堂一间房"到"一家三口一套房"、从"蜗居"到"住有所居"、从鳞次栉比的传统民居到环境优美的现代化住区的沧桑巨变及取得的巨大成就，呈现了全省住房建设者推动住有所居不懈努力的勇气和智慧，折射着中国改革开放大时代的辉煌，具有借鉴和启示未来的作用。

To celebrate the 40th Anniversary of the reform and opening up, we made this short film — *Documentary on the Evolution of Residential Housing in Jiangsu (1978—2017)* to record the achievements of housing development in Jiangsu. With residents' stories, interviews with experts and officials, live action shooting of residential quarters, and clips of housing history records, the film reviews the great changes and achievements of housing development in Jiangsu in the last 40 years since the start of the reform and opening up. From three generations in one room to one apartment for a three-person family, from humble abode to housing accessible to all people, from rows of traditional houses to the beautiful and modern living quarters, all these achievements show the hard work, courage, and wisdom of housing development workers in the province. They are also part of the brilliance in the great era of the reform and opening up in China and inspire us to do better in the future.